SIX YEARS:

A CONDENSATE OF LIFE

March 2017

A Collection

Volume 1

by

Mitchell Ritter

THOUGHTS FROM A FRIEND

I met Mitch close to 10 year ago when he was a recent retournee to New York from Europe. He was looking for a place to live. We connected immediately and formed a friendship. Though we didn't see each other often, when we do, it's like time had hardly passed. It's hard to explain, but then I'm sure he could – that's his thing – understanding the reasons and motivations that lie at the core of our choices, behaviors and lives.

What makes him different – and here I will brieflyborrow his method – was in part the 30 years he lived in Europe. Having to adapt to another culture, another language – in fact many cultures and many languages, raises one's awareness of just how different we all are. Yet in spite of these differences, there are certain universal truths shared across the human experience which transcend culture and bind us all. These are the truth Mitch seeks and the questions he explores.

If you've noticed, to as for real answers – not superficial ones – is often seen as negative and rarely welcome. But when you think about it, that's what makes it all the more important. Without it, we never really step outside ourselves, blinded by so much that conditions our lives individually and collectively Mitch's poetry plays with these very questions, exercising our inner eye.

Take a journey of discovery through mitch's eyes, sensibilities and experiences. Along the way, he help-s provide perspective on just how much we have changed – though few would admit it – and just how it is to see ourselves through the eyes of another.

Mitch creates perspective through his rhythm, rhyme and words. His pointry paints new perspectives, highlighting those things that are so easy to ignore, yet so necessary to know. Each poem propels you forward, taking you on a spiritual journey within yourself.

Enjoy the trip.

KEITH JACOBY
Fine Art
Photography
keithjacoby.com

Table of Contents

THE THEMES

LOVE

Poems about finding, enjoying and losing love. Sweet and simple. Hardly. There are few things we spend more time thinking about, fantasizing about, dreaming about, yet are so ill-prepared, so unaware of the forces operating within us. It was not always so, as in other times, love was not reduced to a matter of biology, chemistry, wiring or instinct. If one takes the time to experience and reflect on the experience, there is much to be learned. Love is perhaps the most complex of experiences we have. Perhaps that's why, lazy as we have become, we prefer to delegate to impersonal forces beyond our capacity to understand or control, rather than become a full participant in one of our defining experiences.

VALUES

Growing up in any place provides us with a set of parameters, or as we used to call them "values." We remain, for the most part, unaware of their existence or their influence, assigning them some obvious, even absolute, authority. Some are led to examine them, rejecting some, embracing others. But many – perhaps too many – lead their lives without ever subjecting those foundational assumptions to   any form of critical thinking. The result? A certain reassuring continuity, until Life intervenes. Confronted with something unanticipated which shatters that certainty, and one discovers that those values may not be sufficient to hold everything together as once thought. Choosing the values we life by is a defining experience and one of Life's true privileges. Here are some observations of just what happens and what is missed - for the individual, their family, and indeed society as a whole - when we take the easy way out.

THE UNLOVED

*I*t is the promise at every new birth that the child will be loved. Sadly, this is not always the case. For those who have grown up in the sun of their parent's care and protection, life will have its challenges, but they will face life with a sense of security and confidence.. For those who grew up in the cold shadow of the moon, Life looks very different. Though they may live next to us, they live behind a mask to hide their loneliness, their hunger and their ever present mistrust. They inhabit another reality where every perception is colored by the expectation of disappointment and betrayal. The injustice of it doesn't escape them, but lacking that fundamental trust, they see no positive way forward. What's left? Revenge. The cost? The future they never believed they truly had. The path? Read on and you will see.

LOSS

*W*e truly live in charmed times when the experience of meaningful loss is often infrequent, and for many, almost entirely absent. Life is   seen   as a straight road towards happiness. And then something happens. An unexpected death, a terrible accident, a cruel illness – all capable of shaking the very foundations of our lives. Who among us has not experienced some form of loss, so painful, so inexplicable, that it changes us forever? There is no measure of the experience as it is perhaps the most personal we encounter.   And there is no anticipating nor preparation for what lies ahead. A dark journey of personal discovery awaits where we confront the ineffable, the randomness of things, our own impotence.   Yet we also learn just how much things that we've lost truly mean to us. It's the essential lesson of Life – all things have an end, so treasure them while you have them. They bring meaning, depth and reason to a chaotic, sometimes cruel, world.

YESTERDAY, TODAY, TOMORROW

Most choose to live in the present, for we are often told not to worry about the past, since it's gone. But is it really? Does each day bring a clean slate where yesterdays are erased and we start fresh? And if today is a new beginning, on what will be base our plans for tomorrow. Or does it mean that tomorrow doesn't really exist, that we the pattern brought you down a good road, all the better. But who doesn't recognize – unwillingly most often – that we tend to make the same mistakes. Perhaps that's why we cling to today, preferring to forget the past and let the future take care of itself. If that's how you see it, ask yourself this. Who is driving the car? You and the conscious   choices you   make? Or some hidden force you choose not to know? And after all, Time is all we really are given. Yet we waste so much of it.......

"I am not what happened to me,
I am what I choose to become."

—Carl Gustav Jung

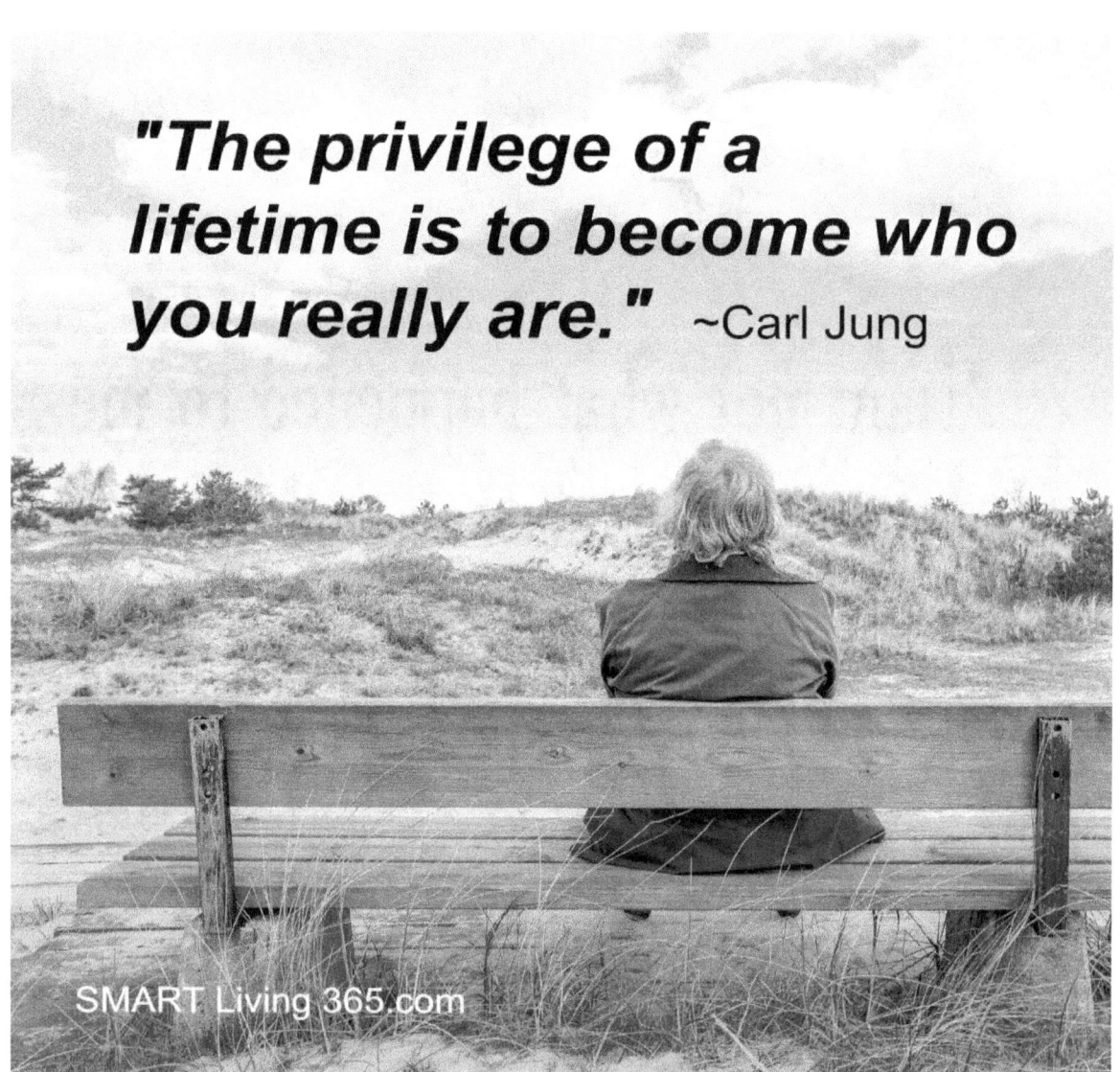

"The privilege of a lifetime is to become who you really are." ~Carl Jung

SMART Living 365.com

ABOUT THE AUTHOR

Mitchell Ritter is a New York City born, Swiss trained clinical (developmental)/Jungian psychologist).   He spent over 30 years living, studying and working in Europe. Returning to New York City in 2002, he has established a private practice on the Upper East Side.   Blessed with two grown daughters, three grandchildren and two large dogs, writing – both prose and poetry - have joined tennis as his favored pastimes.

For further information, please refer to the following website where the author provides insightful quotations and observations on current psychological and social issues drawn from his clinical practice:

www.analyticalpsychologynyc.com

and a website he runs where his interest in poetry finds a broad ranging expression.

www.amazon.com/ebooks/Mr.HidesProgress

'A short story about why people make the wrong decisions.'

www.amazon.com/ebooks/SixYears:AConcentrateofLife

A collection of poems in the "Seussian" style (i.e. Dr. Seuss) derived from observations and experiences from both the author, his patients, and friends. The purpose is to provide perspective and insight into life's challenges and opportunities – welcome ond otherwise.

Comments, thoughts, questions: analyticalpsychologynyc@gmail.com.

ACKNOWLEDGEMENTS

As with my short story, **Mr. Hide's Progress** (also published on Amazon.com/ebooks), this started out without any intention of ever publishing. It was in sharing the manuscript with certain people, and in particular Agustin Iglesias, that I finally decided to make the move. Agustin basically project managed the transition (as he did with Mr. Hide's Progress), and for that I am grateful.

Cover art is always important as it is generally the first thing one notices, and is of particular importance when it comes to something not often sought out as general reading – a poetry collection. But this wasn't meant to be your usual academic, even esoteric, poetry collection. Rather, I hoped for something which could be seen as general reading, a place where one might find – even in concentrated form – come shared experience, a hopeful insight, a way to accept what can't be changed..

As sometimes happens, a chance encounter turns into a solution, and while walking with my dogs in Central Park, I met Brenda Popovitz,* a professional photographer recently arrived in New York, her husband John, and their two dogs. We started talking, and as I described the project, she most graciously offered to help. I think the result captures exactly in a single image, what it took me several thousand words to convey. Thank you.

To the famous Dr. Seuss who gave us so much to consider, 'sneaking' into our consciousness so many essential lessons we tend to forget, and as a children's book – with his eternal freshness, innocence and lack of self-consciousness. I read them as a child. I read them to my children. And one of the first things I did when I was blessed with grandchildren, was to run out and get the same books so I could not only enjoy reading them yet again, but also share those lessons with my grandchildren. He gave me the courage to borrow his deceptively naïve style to impart with purpose, clarity and sincerity questions we all encounter, the answers to which we too often forget how to find. I lack his whimsy – but maybe next time. Since the first encounter, I have been a *Seussian*.

And finally Life herself, for she is an endless source of challenges, lessons, sadness and joy which allows us, if we pay attention and use the minds we were given, to find the necessary measure of wisdom to live our lives as they were intended. I like the old Jewish proverb which says

"...as long as there are 10 good men in the world, it won't come to an end. But they will never know who they are."

*Brenda Popovitz of BKPphoto.com

AUTHOR'S NOTE

*F*or most of my professional life, whether t was in practice or working in industry, I was called upon to write. It was a skill that I honed over the years, striving for concision, structure, clarity and logic. And I was successful. But as time went on, life became more complex, fuller and frankly less about things and more about their depth and texture. I was struck first by the fact that though well written, something was getting in the way of the message getting through. No one seemed to be taking the time to read, asking for the famous "top line," "executive summary," or worse still, the infamous "bullet point."

If the point of communication is to communicate – and there was a time when numbers counted for less than nuance and substance – had to acknowledge that something had changed, and I needed to reevaluate.

Six years ago, there was a significant emotional event in my life which I needed to understand. I tried writing in prose, as was my habit, but I found the linear, efficient logical approach was actually eliminating potentially informative steps. The thinking was there, but where was the emotion? My writing, however "good" – had become professorial, a bit too "knowing," and even a bit boring. The first and essential component of any real connection – in any medium – is emotion. It's the glue that holds the bricks together.

Then it hit me. Aside from Shakespeare and Dr. Seuss, I was neither a reader nor a practitioner of rhyme. Sadly it seems that poetry is considered to be either for children or adults. Yet when are we "taught" poetry? It is usually part of the English curriculum, is taught with no explanation of its power and expressiveness to adolescents who have neither the maturity not the interest to appreciate it. I've come to consider it as a mature art – though it can be taken at the first degree – as a whimsical, somewhat self-indulgent exercise.

At first afraid that my attempts would be clumsy, inarticulate and outright childish, the good doctor (Seuss) came to the rescue. I found my courage. I found a voice. I found new answers began emerging from the journey. For though I knew where I was starting, I never really knew where I would end up, what unsuspected answers might crop up. No longer prisoner of trying to make a point, to convince. Curious, open minded, free from any obligation other than to follow where the words wanted to go.

Once I started, I couldn't stop. I could tackle difficult subjects in an evocative, not an expositive manner, the images were born of the rhyme, and the story from the melody. Self-consciousness became self-confidence. A greater clarity emerged from the collaboration between emotional and reason. And much to my surprise, and in spite of my very un "artful" style, an audience emerged as well.

What follows is a collection of poems I wrote during these past 6 years. They reflect personal experiences, observations, questions – mine or those of others – which have touched me, led me to consider the essential question which we so too often forget to ask – "why?" That's how children start out learning and understanding. Sad that as adults, we often forget just how important that simple word really is

Though arranged by theme, there is no particular order within them. It is often said that we only truly value that which we thought important enough to search for, and once we have found it through our own efforts, it becomes an inseparable part of us. We owe no one a debt, and as these pieces start to come together, we come to own ourselves. Is that not a wonderful thing?

FOR LILY

*T*here are a few poems about Lily, who Death took early and undeservedly. It was one of the worst losses I have ever experienced. Why? Because she was all about love. And when I learned of her illness, I asked her to fight it with all her force – for me. And she did. For four months she endured so much with dignity, and even staged a remarkable rally that amazed all her doctors . And I dared to hope. But Death is a force not to be denied.

Her last night, as she struggled for every breath, I could do nothing but hold her close to me, hoping that the end would come quickly, mercifully. It didn't. At that moment, I thanked her for all she had given me, for fighting because I had asked her to – selfishly. Now it was my turn to give. And I set her free from the promise she had made. And a light went out in the world.

Yes, Lily was a dog – here shown as a puppy, in all her innocence and promise. Almost odd to refer to her as such, for she was possessed with such individuality, such uniqueness, that I think her of her more as Lily than a representative of her species. To do so, as we tend to do with any species other than our own, is to reduce them to lesser creatures. If domination is the principal criterion for superiority, then I guess mankind is indeed at the top of the heap. But in getting there, I can't help wondering if our drive for domination will not reduce the marvel that we have been given to little more than a heap. Then what? Turn on each other?

I dedicate this book to Lily not out of sentimentality. I dedicate it to her for everything she showed me about love, loyalty, dignity and a natural beauty that sadly seems to live mostly in species other than our own. Doing what we do to Nature sometimes seems more an act of vengeance than humanity, for we seem to have lost what others have known better how to preserve. It's the only world we have.

Look into those innocent eyes. Do they not see into your heart? They still do mine.

INTRODUCTION

I have always been a fan of Doctor Seuss. Through deceptively simple tales, fantastical creatures and improbable stories, a certain moral sense unmistakably revealed itself. Never boring, pedantic or professorial. Yet the lessons were important, universal and perhaps most of all, received.

But there was something more to his writing which enabled it to reach so many. Through childlike rhyming and invented words, we were lulled into a state where our usual logical filters simply could not recognize that we were being told something very important. Being thusly captivated, we simply forgot to say no.

With no ambition other than to express myself once again in a fresh, insightful and meaningful way – drawing from observations which are not judgements (the 2 are too often confused in conversation) – my own and those of the people in both my personal and professional lives – I sought to touch that which we all share as part of the human experience, rather than delve into the subjective, the too personal, for communication, to be truly communicative, should benefit not only the person communicating, but hopefully be expressed in such a way as to be meaningful to anyone who is curious enough, open enough, to receive the message..

No. No Dr. Seuss am I.

Yet if my rhymes lead you to ask why/

Perhaps you will be tempted to open more than an eye

And look with joy – curious again - up at the vast blue sky.

SIX YEARS

October 2016

These poems tells of these past six years

Filled with joys, filled with tears

Events unexpected, unwanted, undeserved

Yet punctuated with blessings, life preserved

I saw death in person steal away my heart

I found love, for a time, which played its part

Only to be lost for no good reason

Changes come by themselves, like each new season

My quest for my last great adventure

Only to find each promise met with Life's censure

Like Don Quixote, willing to fight every demon

Though the odds were never even

Ten good men endure, they say, the world to preserve

Ignoring their selection, or why this honor they deserve

Does one have to know the answer now mine?

Or can patience prevail as truth is revealed over time?

We move through space with each step to advance

Whatever wisdom we acquire is it purely by chance?

Do the challenges that are ours, whether chosen of imposed

What matters is how we meet them, doors opened or closed

The years can be kind, providing for our need

Sadly most seek solace in acquisition and greed

What can one learn through accumulation?

What do we become – ourselves, our nation?

These past six years have been in experience rich

The clock ticking only exaggerates the itch

Time is all we are truly given

To learn what we can before from this world we are riven

I've had the chance to taste life in so many ways

New perspectives have come to fill my days

To seek order in worlds both inner and external

Hoping to find the answers to things eternal

For money, power, adulation and such

On my last day they won't amount to much

All the things I thought important were nothing but a crutch

What will count on that day, when all is said and done, is the lives I've been able to touch

To share what I've learned, for what it's worth

The well spent hours of reflection, and not their dearth

The reward – at least for now as I see it – is some inner peace

No fear, no anxiety, but depth and connection – release.

For if death is the endpoint – as unavoidable as I've seen

That ghostly man who comes in the night, his presence ethereal yet keen

Devoid of passion, he sucks the very life from a child

To watch him work, though his manner be mild

To see beauty taken undeservedly too soon

To live in a world without sun, but only a moon

Cold and empty, left to wonder why

Such goodness withdrawn leaving only an empty black sky

I've wandered this dark place in search of some light

Is there some point to rising up and continue the fight?

Give up or live on, for the past or what is still to come?

Perhaps over the next hill will rise the sun

No homelies have I learned to ease the pain

No seven stages of grief can erase the stain

But the heart is meant to heal

As we are all meant to feel.

So read on of the joys and the tears

Feel your heart lighten, dispel the fears

Taken together – experience can bring some completeness of sight

No more old demons or fears, but the courage and reason to continue the fight.

Not some combat in the traditional sense

The weapons aren't lethal or some absurd fence.

Life is a struggle, being its own true reward

What you make of it, if you've found your path, move forward.

If you arrive at the end or not counts for naught

Just be sure to learn and to share what you were taught.

Evil and Good define this world of ours

Each having its own special powers

One came first, it's from him we are born

The second came with a purpose, as if from the mud torn

For he points to sky, revealing what we can be

If we lift our eyes up so we can see

Choices define us, the ones that we make

The second says to give, the first to take

Which will you be? How will you choose?

That's what will decide if in Life you win or lose.

LOVE

BIRTHDAY

April 2013

The end of March is fast approaching

The time left to me to write is fast encroaching

I think of you often – as much for me as for you

Still not sure who is getting what they are due,

I write for myself, stolen moments from the past

Refusing to abandon that which I wanted so much to last

Subjective these thoughts, the emotions endure

They bring solace but alas no final cure,

I wonder still what use you make of my verse

Do they make you feel better, or do they make you feel worse?

I hope for the former, for love wants only the best

But within this feeling resides a necessary test

One that will always challenge you in ways your abhor

For reasons I've spoken of often, no need to further explore

A conundrum, a dilemma, a knot with no end

And yet these messages I continue to send.

Is it a gestation, a period of invisible growth?

For me or you or better yet, both

qA port of call, a safe haven, a home

Safe from the waters and their surging foam.

Was it a dream, a lie, a figment of mine?

I've looked deep within for some clarifying sign

But certainty of this type I do not own

It can't be defined by one person all alone

The answer requires, like some complex equation

A lengthy process of elucidation

No shortcuts, no steps skipped, no easy solution

Each operation depends on what came before for its final resolution.

So where are we in this process, complex and long

Am I alone to hear the melody which precedes the song,

I play my part as my heart guides my way

For a time I am silent until I have something to say

But keep this alive for purposes perhaps unclear

I won't let it yet die, so I keep you near

It gives me hope that love does exist

Even if its path holds many a twist

A symbol of what it feels like to care

Whoever said love was supposed to be fair?

So as your third decade draws to a close

As you look back on the pathways you chose

Have the seeds I've planted taken root?

Have you found nourishment from them like some precious fruit?

Has the baby inside you, the new you waiting to be born

Is your hair still growing, or have you had it shorn?

Have you allowed yourself more clearly to see?

Have you found a way to bring forward what you want to be?

So on this day of your 39 years

Are you still imprisoned by your fears?

That you cannot be who you are

Have you been able to see that far?

These things I send, my gifts to you

You are more special than you think......if only you knew.

WHAT'S IN A TOUCH?

May 5, 2012

What's in a touch that it can mean so much?

That the language it speaks evokes such peaks

Of physical desire and spiritual fire

What's in a kiss that it brings such bliss?

With words unspoken

Promises unbroken

Articulate yet mute

Speaks in the silvery tones of a flute

What's in a face

That it makes a heart race?

All come together, the present tense

Step out of time and into sense

What's in the eyes?

The truth, not lies.

No secrets long therein to hide

Together, side by side

Aquamarine, limpid and clear

In the moment, no place for fear.

What's in the heart

That it breaks when apart?

A place, a home, the central core

No need to question any more.

What is it about love

That makes us rise above?

When doubts fade and all becomes clear

When answers replace questions, not far but near

What is a man?

But all that he can?

When the measure of his strength

Is the sense he can go to any length

Where do these feelings live when not given voice?

What do they do when they have no choice?

Do they go away never to return?

Or in some hidden fire do they continue to burn?

Will they die like some consumed ember?

Or do they grow in strength, denied, but alive forever?

As waste do they perish forgotten and lost?

And if that's what happens, is there a cost?

Should we abandon that which we love?

Or hold on to it dearly, like a hand in a glove?

For such is the fullness once it is found.

Two hearts together as one, forever bound?

Is this a dream or can it be real?

it endure? Some sacred pact to seal?

Or is it meant to come and go?

Or is it a seed destined to grow?

Choice or compromise, is that life's equation?

The former a promise, the second a negation

Of that which is pure, true and rich

Substitution no option, this is one thing one that cannot switch

Like a muse from whom the music flows

The seed takes root, prospers and grows

Perhaps other melodies can be found

As one hungry heart search o'er the ground

Other music to make, other voices to be joined

New songs to be sung, new titles coined

And though they may help us live life through our time

Each with its distinctive taste like some fine wine

The source, once found, remains at the heart of it all

Never deaf to the sweet sound of the call

But silence is a prison built by thine own hand

Its walls high, forbidding, yet rooted only in sand

Though fooled to believe it will ever last

The day will come when the die, long ago cast

Will bring down those blocks heavy and dead

Revealing that which has long been dread.

What now to do with the truth revealed?

What of the wound neglected that never healed?

The sight of which so long ago hidden

Gaze into the eyes of the forbidden

What will you see when you can no longer look away?

Will you step from the ashes, run once again or stay?

But where to go once all roads have disappeared

Save one, the true one, the one most feared

But why fear that which is true?

How did you get so lost in you?

The story has been told again and again

Of late and too often by this stubborn pen

Embrace at last what you can no longer ignore

Courage in hand, go through the door.

Leave the ruins finally seen for what they are

Dead, empty, and sticky, a pit of tar

Resume the journey you were meant to take

Be real at last, no longer fake

No false expression, no deceptive smile

No playful charm like some carefree child

No baggage weighing you down

A smile no longer required to hide the frown

It begins and ends in the same place

When you can look yourself in your face

When those eyes of aquamarine

Look to the future, wizened by what they've seen

TOO WELL HEALED

November 21, 2014

Here I stand, my shame revealed

One part still wounded, the other healed

In normal times, this would suffice

The two would meld into one at no additional price.

But this time it's different, the rift remains

And I have not found the way to stop covering my days with stains

Of disappointment, in failure, a sense of loss

I must acknowledge I am no longer – perhaps never was - the boss.

A conflict has seized me, a problem to solve

Though still strong, I doubt my failing resolve

For when I am called and have a choice

Reason gives way to want, it has not the voice\

To speak in ways beyond the words

The phrases fly away like frightened birds.

And what remains, some demon base

My vision fails, a lie I chase

Though it brings a moment's reprieve

Once over, I shake my head, and begin again to grieve.

What is this sadness that drives me so?

It has a name, one I know

Yet foreign it feels, this is not me

One look informs for all to see.

But wait, perhaps the wound healed too well

It hides a darker truth, one it must tell

Of a time when alone was all around

Its silence was the only sound

And none more fearful, louder than any din

Blamed myself, embraced my sin.

And though I know I have done what I could

How much really has it helped, was it right and good?

For sure I have forged ahead and built a life

Had children along the way, and lost a wife.

That's the truth, the riddle, the problem stares me in the face

What to do as I round the corner and head on to finish the race?

So much to give still lives inside my heart

Its piled high, unwieldy, like some overloaded cart

I push it forward, the only direction I know

Spilling seeds of care in the hope to see one grow.

But this land has grown sterile, none take deep root

Unfelt by others they are trampled under a selfish boot

So what to do, for only half can I control

Just keep on trying and with the punches roll.

That's no longer an answer that can endure

I need to look deeper to find some cure

Abandon my quest, accept my fate

Since struggling only seems to shut the gate.

Is the scar too perfect, hiding some darker truth?

Instead of suave and smooth, have I hidden something uncouth?

Too perfect, to clean, where nothing can stick

A wound too well healed can prove too slick.

Where there are no rough edges for another to fix upon

Is that why so many have come and gone?

AMBIVALENCE

July 2016

Some say that we live in simple world of black and white

It's this or it's that, just pick one, why fight?

Like love or hate, you or me

Presented this way – easy to see.

Then why is it so many can't seem to decide?

They go through life confused, unable to choose, running on glide

Where is the steering wheel and that pedal to accelerate?

To see our goal and head straight for the gate.

It can feel as though things make no sense

Chaos prevails, too thick, too dense

Why risk charging towards who knows what or who?

Not sure why you're afraid, courage seems to reside in only so few

A mistake, a rejection, do they deserve the respect they've received?

Or have we become befuddled, fearful, deceived?

And thinking, that skill we used to cherish

Too hard, too long, and if I take a stand, might I even perish?

Childish fears when considered from afar

So how did this happen, who stripped down the car?

I think this world of opposites seemingly clear

This shorthand of steps skipped has resulted in some vague fear

Intuition tells us the picture is incomplete

Once again without thinking, we are satisfied to just dip in our feet

Not to get wet, that would look like taking a stand

Who wants to be alone in a crowd where no one extends a hand?

So we live in a land where only the in-between exists

Where no road is straight but made up of turns and twists

They confuse me, they frighten, and ultimately I find myself lost

No longer knowing what to think – a terrible cost

I pretend to see both sides, each appearing right

How could I be sure, to thread the needle with that tiny hole so tight?

A mistake – dear Lord – me? To be wrong?

If I'm as perfect as I've been told, that wouldn't be my song

But how else do we learn, really understand

It's not something innate like an organ or a gland

It's character, the result of choices we make

How could we always be right if no risks we take?

And if we fall, if it all falls down

No one will kill us or chase us from town

Consequences are required to become a man

Sometimes its necessary to jump into the fire from out of the pan

It burns, we may suffer, yet discover an unsuspected strength

I can survive these trials and continue my journey one more length.

In truth, there is honesty in not holding back

Others, non-subscribers, remain unaware of what they lack

Lost, stuck, unhappy yet unable to move

They live in a rut having lost their groove.

Clarity comes only from looking within

To find what's really important and focus, we begin

Purpose, direction, a sense of self starts to emerge

And long lost desires resurface – a healthy urge

To actually want someone without doubt or fear

What they bring to our lives is simple and clear

Ambivalence is that place where all is confused and drear

Where the strongest emotions are doubt and fear

Where courage and daring and risk no longer exist

Where flight is the answer, have we forgotten how to make a fist?

To say to Life "you may win in the end"

The winds may blow and the obstacles make me bend

But as long as I know what is important, these seas I can sail

I may not get the prize in the end, but I cannot fail.

THE FOREST

I entered the forest looking for gold

Trust and caring, new rules to hold

Was it a dream, an illusion, or a reach too bold?

A fantasy of youth I chase as I grow old?

Were its benefits oversold?

Dare I let the dream go cold?

The forest of trees is made

Structure, order within is forbade

Yet used to science, logic and more

Illusions to make us believe we can know what's in store

The primal forest, trees helter skelter

Designed to confuse more than to shelter

Another illusion for in times gone by

It meant something else, the unknown for us to try

For food, for fire, for clothes and more

Was she a mother or was she a whore?

Perhaps she was both, unbeknownst to us

Each time we entered, what was the fuss?

A decade ago, where has time gone by

I entered the forest, my luck to try

Encounters of all sorts, both good and bad

Thinking I made progress, never truly sad

For I believed that somehow sense it all made

And so to my chosen course I stayed

There were days when it felt right and true

And there were days when more than the sky was blue

Yet hope carried me, one step then another

As in the myths of times past, seeking the faithful other

The one who would know which fork to take

The bonds of friendship, a life to make

Yet the order of the trees I no longer see

With clearer vision, it makes less sense to me

The irony of knowledge, experience and such

Is in the end, we really don't know that much

Surely not enough, the future to know

Or what it really means to grow.

I look at the forest and see the trees

Seduced by their beauty, I drop to my knees

But no longer can I look dumbly at nature and say

If I look hard enough I will surely know the way

So lost in the trees with meager tools

I sort through those encountered, few wise; mostly fools

I've been here before, and reasoned it all

Clung steadfast to a branch so I won't fall.

I look at the trees and see their shape

Rectilinear, from order they all escape

A tree stands up straight, but only if not broken

Spared by nature, a generous token

Its' branches reach out, as if some hope to grasp

To stif it had hands, it would clasp

Hold fast to whatever offered strength and support

Safe like a ship in a protected port

Held firmly in place by chains and rope

Through the storms this is how it will survive and cope

But branches don't grasp, the reach for the sun

Searching the light for strength, they only stand, can't run

Is that why they spread in random order?

No obvious lines, limits, purpose, or border

But I have legs and the will to search

And though through this maze I struggle, I lurch

Fooled too often by what resembled a road

Uncertain, keep moving, myself I goad

Yet what do I see, what lies ahead?

More trees, more forest, no roof, no bed

There is a beginning, there is an end

Another illusion, more hope to send?

But wait, we forget, way back in time

The forest knew no limits, no borders, no line

Have we, in our haste to make sense of it all

Created a fallacy that promises much, but guaranteeing more likely a fall.

How many times to pick ourselves up?

How many times can one glue back the pieces of the broken cup?

I know the answer, at least for now

We have a choice ourselves to allow

Continue to seek out that which we need

Be mindful of that which wounds us and makes us bleed

It can be avoided, at times, if we look with our heart

One eye on the road, the

And in the end, who knows if sense and order exist

To find out, all we can do is persist.

EACH STEP

April 2010

Friday after tennis, shaken was your world

Into zones intempestuous you felt yourself hurled

Such harsh thoughts garnered, surrounding you

Chased the sun, left the sky a murky blue

Such pain, such solitude, such doubt undeserved

Cure it my love could not, however unreserved

Difficult to watch you struggle as I know you did

Your heart you showed me, it no longer hid

My pain for you, felt as I watch you hurt

With yourself the issues you do not skirt

Too harsh, too mean, too sharp, too raw

How to change this thing at your heart which does gnaw?'

And yet, through your battles, I see progress you make

I feel your love, with each step that you take

Victory now - not the essential part

Feed your dreams, yourself, your love, your heart

The battle is engaged, this I know

I've watched you these months new seeds to sow.

Progress never comes in a straight line

But strong and tall these seeds can grow over time

Prevail you will, though now you may doubt

When your heart aches and your head knows not what it's all about

One step at a time, even backwards you think you may go

Nothing can stop you, this I know

For you can love, I've tasted its glory

If you allow it - with great struggle - to rewrite its story

A tale long ago distorted, twisted into something wrong

Yet listen to the music you hear emerging, it's your truer song

A cost I bear, a twofold bill

See you in pain then miss you still

Through our time together, I've learned to see beyond

The shallow waters of my subjective pond.

You've given me a new reason to think beyond myself

To see something bigger than some self-absorbed elf

The one who in his self-pitying misfortune wallowed

Into some solitary place, alone, sad, I let myself be swallowed

Having you in my life, a better focus I found

A glorious ship, part of who was momentarily stuck in the ground

Take my love, my experience and whatever else of value I may have

To see you rise in the waters, your sails fill with wind, your heart to save

And in so doing, if you will allow me so

I too learn, love, prosper and grow

For the day will come when need you too I will

When in sorrow my own heart will need a refill

But together, as one, two stronger for sure

My ship, she of such beauteous allure

Will lift me up, when aground I may be

And carry me onwards to a calmer sea.

Return to your cave in these moments so dark

Live on stale water and cast off bark

If sustain you they have o'er these past many years

Then be grateful for their service, they allayed your faceless fears

But your life has changed, with new promise it's filled

The bear must seek refuge elsewhere, new fields call to be tilled

Not in the dark sad place from before

But in the sunlight, proud, happy, loved - that's what's in store.

These voices which turn good to bad

Which steal your smile and make you sad

Chase them away, see them for what they are

Cast them adrift, to float off to some foreign space afar

Friends they are not. Demons they be

Distorting your thoughts and emotions, so as not to see

Using tricks of deception, doubt, confusion and fear

To keep you theirs and hold you near.

Ghosts from the past these dark gnomes of doubt

Whose hold on you they will soon be without

For once they are seen for who they be

They'll be put in a jar and drowned in the sea.

Words from the future, tonight you may say

Not believing that yet has arrived that day

But the sun will rise, its light will fill your eyes

The only sound you'll hear, much relieved sighs.

So do what you must now, do what you can

Know that you have no greater fan

Let me be your light, your knight, your hope

As through the darker moments you grope

I've no need to ask for promises unsound

For I know that which I have found

Your way you will find to a better place

And there, next to me will be awaiting your well earned place.

REJOICE

October 13, 2012

Though we were together for only a short time

Seven months was all when you were really only partly mine

When your darker truth you hid from both our eyes

The words you spoke, the things you did created ties

They have resisted these two years

And a secret place in my heart still sheds tears

I gave them voice thinking to empty the well

And hoped in your story to tell

That some fuller truth I might find

So these bonds to somehow unwind

I've reasoned myself and understood

Separated the bad from the good

Seen clearly, and spoke in words of love and care

And though I carry on, outwardly balanced and fair

When foul winds blow me away from some friendly port

A place to rest, to find joy, to love, to cavort

It's back to you I seem to float

I can change my sails, my tillar, but not my boat.

This is no obsession, harsh or unkind

Nor the work from some dark corner of my mind

Love speaks its truth and will not give up

The precious liquid which once filled its cup.

Back and forth, from hurt to heal

When most of all I need to feel

The life which flows from its deepest source

I cannot deviate from my course.

Some say that once in life we feel a connection such as this

When nothing but you can bring such bliss

I weaken at times thinking of you

And slide backwards to who I loved, who I knew.

And from that dark place I no longer seek

A glimmer of light, some days, I allow to peek

That what we shared still within you lives

Growing slowly but surely, more courage it gives.

Not waiting for some miraculous cure

But like gold from lead, creating something pure

The seed takes shape, possesses its host

Chasing evil demons, past ghosts.

And at the end, if what I believe to be true

What will remain is my you.

And that day, should it come to be

My bell will ring, you will come to me.

And on that day, I will rejoice

You were reborn and finally made the right choice.

REACHING YOU

How do I reach you?

How do I teach you?

How do I show you the way ahead?

What words of magic can possibly be said?

This fire that burns deep inside

The feelings I have for you still, I don't care to hide

You inhabit my space, my mind and my heart

I think of you too often to make sense of us being apart.

Obsession. No – it's not about that

That would be the interpretation, an explanation too pat

Love lives inside me, all else pales when compared

Your face, your body, your lips, naked inside you we dared.

That's the reason, if only this bond

Could be tossed overboard, drowned in some pond

I've come to understand your fear, your fate

Try though I do, I can feel no hate.

Frustration, anger, impatience, though no disgust

My hunger for you derives from some primal lust

So much in common, yet so far apart in ways

A gap you have left in all of my days.

Sleep with others, try though I do

No love can I feel for them, not like with you

Do you feel the same? I think it's so

Or else why would you run from me, and all that I know

About your soul, your body and your heart

The sweetness, the fullness, the joy fill the cart

But you are stuck in the past, afraid to look out.

I rant, I rave, I scream, I shout.

Hear me you do – of that I'm sure

Does your love for me, in spite of it all, still endure?

Free me from this, abandon your flight

Talk to me, look at me, touch me – back in my world alight.

Reason tells me, nothing to do

Think of myself, focus on the negative, destroy the memory of you

But as I've told you many a time

Destroy a love, in my world, is the greatest crime.

Look around you. Where love do you see?

When in your life have you ever felt so free?

Though brief moments were followed by confusion and pain

Stay true to your word, come back to me again.

Move on. Turn the page. Find someone else, better than you

Take the wheel, change the course, leave behind me this bitter brew

Let time do its work, no pain can you I spare

No matter how much I love, no matter how much I care

Like some parent watching a child find its way

Needing to stumble, fall and ultimately pay

Salvation comes at a price too high

When all I can do is watch from a distance, and deeply sigh

I've thrown all I have at you, perhaps an approach all wrong

But that's what I know how to do, that's my vision of strong

But yours is different, immature and unformed

Bring down your defenses I can't, though their walls I have stormed.

No answer have I found, as yet, to touch again your emprisoned heart

Your past keeps you captive, and us apart

If only you could look to the future with hope

You'd see that with love, you'd do more than just cope.

Survival's your way, how you view your life

As you inhabit that prison in your role as a wife

No sex. No joy. No love. Only shadows from times gone by

Together they form this hateful lie.

Send this today – best to wait?

To leave you alone to digest the mountain I've put on your plate

Trust that you, more clearly will see

What lies ahead with him, or with me.

Do you still fear losing yourself to love?

Do you believe that only through control and a sterile partner you can remain above?

To live an air, so thin and spare

To never feel love again, no passion, no care

The absence of problems, the simple life

Attractive it seems, free from emotional strife.

How to deal with your feelings, understand them, draw from their strength

To avoid this discovery, you go to great lengths

Always the no, rarely a yes allowed

Keep your heart imprisioned, your spirit "cool" but cowed.

Such fullness, such potential, all the promises denied

Lead you down a path when all your words are lied

Does this not tell you the wrong path you are on?

Your immature friends need to be gone

Put yourself in a place where you can grow

Where you can see, feel, hear, speak and know

Ignorance chosen, not only evil and dire

Like throwing the knowledge of books in some great fire

Ideas. Feelings. Love. And wisdom too

Can only be deferred. The needs they come from will rise anew.

Wait longer, postpone, hide, ignore

Once opened, you cannot forever again shut the door

Futile. Destructive. A Luddite's embrace

This is the world you are building, the disease, the case

If Nadal or Roger approached their game this way

Would they ever progress? Would they ever hold sway?

Risks must be taken, life lived without doubt

Makes for a life of emptiness, no values or what we're about

Cling to your security, like some buoy on a sea, adrift

Is that how you see yourself, no friendly hand you to lift?

You know there is one, strong and true

Who wants only to be there for you

.

To give what he has that is in him, the best

So you can overcome this dark knot that constricts your chest.

Breathe deeply. Fill your soul

Become all that you can, that is the goal

Let me be there, a part of this

And feel once again, my tender, loving, warm kiss....

SUNSHINE/NO CURE

April 2, 2012

Is there a point, is there a way?

To keep one's faith in another day

That all the hope placed in another's heart

Will I see them rise up and assume their part?

Is it a fantasy nourished in vain?

One that seems to soothe, but also grows in pain

For to believe in something that will not be

Is to close one's eyes to what is clear to see

The dilemma of faith, wherever it's placed

Is the same, but I wonder to which source can it be traced

Why do some need to hold on to that which appears lost?

Do they not see the ultimate cost?

Is it only about getting through another day?

Bridging some void, today's loneliness held at bay

Is faith about taking oneself out of time?

And when unfulfilled, is it the punishment or the crime?

Some trick of the mind as we wait for salvation

Residing down here in our faithless nation

Is it another of life's enigmatic ploys?

As we search in the dark are we merely one of chaos' toys?

A choice, some would say, we have to make

Leading us forward as in our lives we build our stake

Is that the point, defining our values, our way?

Is this the only means of truly having our say?

Regardless the outcome, though the lottery some do win

Is this how we keep ourselves safe from sin?

Is it all about forging morality's rule?

As we long for the fourth leg of this three legged stool?

We hope for an answer, some truth rooted deep

From confusion secure is this how safe we keep?

The alternative, is it too frightening to consider?

Is it all a gamble, and are we the blind bidder?

Questions without answers, is that what this is about?

To wander blindfolded, brave-hearted and stout

There are days when I believe that it will all come true

When I look up at the sky and speak my heart to You

What form will the answer take, if it comes at all?

Am I setting myself up by believing to trip and fall?

And if I see sense where there is none to be found

As I look to the sky, ignoring the holes in the ground

Will I surely fall in one and land on my face?

Is the sole purpose simply to pick myself up and get back in the race?

Metaphorically speaking, past wisdom does reveal

Answers rational, even clever, but how real?

My mood will determine my view of events

Do I pack it up or pitch my tent?

One day sense appears, my waiting finds its reward

My life, like some ship, ready to sail, all aboard

Another day comes, disappointments abound

I listen for the sweet music of your voice, but hear no a sound

What to think? The first stop of the mind

Is Life evil and "care" less or is she kind?

Is someone out there watching over me?

It seems not today, only treachery

Unintended, yet cruel, robbing me of my faith

Was it an angel or some evil wraith?

As experience grows and we seek to understand

Are we building on solid ground or shifting sand?

Is this thing I pursue, this wisdom I seek

Is it written in English, French or Greek?

Someday I may glean and understand well

Much remains too unclear for me to tell

As I approach some inevitable end

Will I find good news or only an obituary to send?

To be remembered for a short moment in time

Then forgotten with no one my loss to pine

And even if that were the case

Is that what I'd want to take my place?

Today is a day of darker emotion

The sea is murky, a turgid ocean

Another day will come, of that I'm sure

Perhaps it will bring some sunshine, if not a cure.

THE MUSE – HAPPY BIRTHDAY

As you've probably noted

And with no ill intent

I've been using you

And it's all been sent

What I've discovered through these many months of thought

A gift was acquired, with pain it was bought

But a gift nonetheless, a new means in my life

Like the tennis you reintroduced brought me more than the too familiar strife

But what might I owe you in exchange for this gift?

One that provided to my life such a lift

Was the debt not paid well in advance?

For a new opening in your life, much insight, and more than a second chance

Even if no sprouts have yet appeared

A potential way forward to you has been cleared.

A muse serves a purpose, clear and strong

Providing direction, a path to walk along

Preferably together, but alone for a time, if such is required

As long as what is learned is shared, one moving ahead, the other still mired

In issues of the past, unaddressed, unresolved

The sin remains for both, unabsolved

But a muse is a wonder, a soul to enjoy

To be played with and discovered, with great care, not some pointless toy

And so for me, caring I remain

Perhaps as a gift, perhaps an enduring stain

One that won't go away, annoying at times, harsh

A hand always offered to pull you out from the marsh

Is it abuse, this thing so real?

Does it still hurt when you start to feel?

Whose purpose does it really serve?

Is it a straight line or a perilous curve?

Clearly depending on one's point of view

It has helped me. Have you let it do as much for you?

Two sides of you I've seen over time

Before you returned to your cell, when you were still mine

One true, the other unsure

I believed in the first, innocent and pure

That word abuse, I used it near our end

I chose it carefully, a multi-layered message to send

How are you I wonder from time to time

Have you found your way out of the crime

Are you feeling better, are you doing ok?

Has anything changed? Have you altered your way?

I've been through tough times the past weeks three or four

And when that happens, at times – like you – I shut the door

Anger fills my heart, a defensive wall built high and strong

Safe inside my fortress of solitude, for awhile, I believe there I belong

Why open my heart to the faithless mass?

How could I believe when like ships in the night, through my life they pass?

In these moments of pain, thoughts of you return

For as he remade you, with you I've come to learn

Some innocence was lost along the way

So many unanswered words, yet true to my heart I stay

More difficult now to believe when so little proof is to be found

Though my words speak the truth, others deaf to their hearts, hear no sound

As your birthday approaches, I've wondered what to do

Should I cease and desist or continue?

I rely on my muse, for that's where the words spring from

I cannot force them, from such a special place they come

No more lessons I feel I need to provide

I've planted a naked seed in you, now we must wait and see if it will grow and divide

I've showered you with caring and affection, like the rain and the sun

This seed, will it take root, or will you continue to run

Thirty eight, the number grows closer to a milestone for sure

Will the disease continue to spread, or will there be a cure?

Will you step up and become the one I believe that you are?

The one whose journey should lead them far.

I watch from a distance now, no longer feeling the pain

The stakes have changed, I have no new refrain

Of late a wise friend asked me if you were the love of my life

Did I still want you for my "wife"

Aside from the word, chosen in haste

I pondered the question, sampled its taste

I feel you further now, no longer filling my world

Though none has come along their banner unfurled

I wander there, if as in the past

Have the dice been thrown, has the dye been cast?

If you were but a transitional step

Surely I'd have met another to be kept

Though I've sampled so many and left them all behind

Perhaps you and I, we're two of a kind

No more answers have I, but freer now I feel

I struggle to discern that which is fake from that which is real

One conviction remains, unshaken and sure

What we shared was true, innocent and pure

So who knows what the future will hold?

Will it be meek or will it be bold?

My journey has taken the latter road

Am I a prince or am I a toad?

I know now I hold only half the equation

Is there another to complete me in this faithless nation?

My search continues as I try to see

Is there an answer and will it someday find me?

But on this occasion, this day of your birth

A day I've described before as one of joy and mirth

My thoughts turn to you once again

Compelled by my muse, to pick up my pen

I watch but don't wait, no longer jump at 9.30 sharp

The text bell on my phone no longer some heavenly harp

Announcing a greeting for the new day

Will there be clouds or will my Sunshine stay

Feel what you can when this you read

Feel life coursing through you, not some draining bleed

Feel the vessel that is your heart come alive

And look to a brighter future, one for which you can strive

Life hasn't beaten you though this you believe

Rejoice in the wonder of you, see what I see, no longer grieve.

Believe in you I always will

This faith I have you cannot kill

On this special day, it's my gift to you

Hold it close, that which you always knew

Like us in this world there may be only a few.

TENDERNESS

June 18, 2013

How do you live without tenderness?

When the world surrounding us is such a mess

Where do you go to renew your strength?

When you've reached the end of your rope and there is no more length

Do you look around you? What do you see?

Is there anything there that makes you be?

That makes you feel alive the way you once did

When you felt the surge of youth, when you were a kid

When the world was new and hope did abound

Before your ship had run aground

When dreams flowed naturally from deep in your heart

When you felt you belonged, not like now, somehow apart

Tenderness, the key to the door within

Which washes us clean of each and every sin

To rise from a bed shared together

Strong enough to face any weather

Now these are images tarnished from neglect

Hearts nowadays know no respect

Only fantasy serves as a guide to the true north

Which is why so few dare to venture forth

For imagined emotions serve only one master

A mirror image of oneself alone makes the heart beat faster

But put someone real and a stranger appears

And arise once again all those ancient fears

So run and hide, disappear, dissolve

The timid live in caves, they have no resolve

To peek out into the light from time to time

Hoping to see salvation's sign

But every glimmer of light promising new hope

Tests the mettle, with a true reality can they cope?

Or is the cave's darkness, familiar and cold

Enough to scare the fearful, chasing the bold

What's happened to us, how have we changed in this way?

When the mind's fancy has silenced the heart's ability to say

To speak its truth, to take a stand

To look at life, and to another, and extend a brave hand.

ALCHEMY

Two separate vessels, existing alone

Searching for something that will bring them home

A process of purification first required

In baggage from the past their feet remain mired

How to proceed, the path to freedom resides where?

How to open the doors wide, free, to care?

The answer, a process, at times painful and long

With highs and lows, like some beautiful song

A connection found, points first the way

As differences emerge, make it harder to stay

But that is the point, the reason, the road ahead

These differences, at first weigh heavy like lead

As obstacles, a loss of identity may appear

The way forward no longer looks quite so clear

It winds, it turns, with ups and downs

Mixing days made of smiles, with days made of frowns

What's the source, turning joy to pain?

Why is the road paved like this, where is the gain?

Emotions, feelings, like wood for some fire

Produce strong moments, confusion, sometimes ire

But these two vessels, separate and apart

Together they form one crucible, one zone, a shared heart

Within it we pour our past, issues and fears

Hoping, yet frightened, what awaits once the smoke clears?

As the fire consumes, separating solid from smoke

Burning away the impurities which otherwise our future would choke

The heat of emotion, conflict, even anger so strange

Is what will free us to join, our future, unencumbered to arrange.

I've spoken to you before of fear, of doubt

Never underestimate their negative clout

Look beyond the immediate, though disregard it not

The emotion provides the heat, cooks the meal, warms the pot

Differences are blended, transformed into something new

Something richer, deeper, more meaningful, a magical brew

Purpose becomes clear, fears abate

Set before us a wondrous meal on a golden plate

Strange it may seem to you, even causing you pain

Struggle is a necessary part of the gain

We earn our rewards, paying for them gives them worth

But in so doing we own our home, our heart, our berth

I love you, desire you, want you in my life

Suffer as well do I, enduring the strife

But I know that through this we must first go

If a life together, if it is to be so

This I want and gladly pay the price

Through days of love and lonely nights

Believe in you, you won't keep us apart

Trusting you and in your brave heart

Time may seem like some evil foe

Forcing me to hold in check my love, not let it grow

For my heart is full, wild and aflame

Blinding me at times, like some runaway train

But the path, the tracks, they are nailed to the ground

Their direction, their purpose, their worth are all sound

Help me, engage your demons past

Let's build together something that will truly last.

THE SWAN'S HEART

2012

There are days when I wonder if writing in verse

Makes things better or makes them worse

I have always thought that the heart should speak

If I gave it voice, it would make me strong, not weak

It's true that like some bottomless spring

Like a bird, once set free, by itself would take wing

Though I find release in the words which flow on their own

I wonder if in so doing, the hole in my heart has not grown

For it is full, of that there is no doubt

But to whom is given the greater clout?

I feel, of that I am sure

And the love that emerges appears innocent and pure

But the more I indulge this passion of mine

The pressure inside devours my house like some vine

Instead of truly setting me free

I feel more bound to this fertile ground like some tree

Immobile, forbidden to move on to love another

Why is my heart held captive by this faithless other?

Not through some force of my own volition

Not through some convention or tradition

Should not release empty the vessel?

Rather with these emotions I continue to wrestle

More than a year and half since we've shared

More than a year and a half since you dared

More than a year and a half have I fought

More than a year and a half have I sought

Some answers, some words, some means to move on

But always returning like some too faithful swan

Those who mate for life, come what may

Never leaving, always having to stay

Have I lost sight of who you really are?

Have I raised too high for some, yet for you lowered, the bar?

To a point where pass you always will

Will my heart never be relieved from this unrelenting fill?

The cap that held captive this primal source

Has not survived the intemperate divorce

Like life's waters, my emotions continue to rise

An endless source seeking only their prize

The one who they'll bathe, cleanse and nourish

Together as one, forever to cherish

I have tried to discipline myself to little avail

Back to you, it seems, leads every trail

Is this some maze from which there is no escape?

Do I seal my eyes shut with some invisible tape?

The more I feel, the clearer I think I see

Yet no peace endures and lets me be

I write to relieve the tide always rising up

It seems love's chalice can't be emptied, forever refilling this precious cup

But I see with my heart and not my eyes

Fruitless attempts over so many tries

o I pursue the many whose paths I cross

For a time I feel fulfilled, but then returns the sense of loss

Days may go by when relief I find

When thoughts of you do not fill my mind

But out of nowhere comes some reminder

If only you were more caring, and kinder

But no, the more I write, I've came to know

A familiar sunshine, a warming glow

For in our short time from a small seed a tree did grow

In the face of all forces and strong winds that blow

Tear it out from the ground, cut it down?

Burn the wood, fill the hole, speak no more of it – shut it down?

Can such violence end what was perhaps meant to be?

Can killing life's roots ensure future vitality?

But what if it's more about wanting something too much?

Can lies be told by a body, a touch?

No - they come more readily from words than a kiss

Is the disorder of it all what keeps me in this?

In this mission, this quest, this unremitting way

I continue to have so much to say

At times it seems I only repeat my words

Together do they form an altar or just a pile of turds?

You'd probably prefer the latter, such is your way

You'd be free to run rather than to think, to stay

But for me, if they return, it's to speak the truth

Innocent. Pure. Articulate. Nothing uncouth

So for now, after this sidetrip, I return to my way

Filled with a search for new loves and a new day

Will you free me – can you let me go?

That's not what you want – this I know.

How long will I be held in place by your power of no?

Like some dead wall with nowhere to go?

The one you've invoked to everyone's loss

Control thusly abused does not make you the boss

Of you or me or anyone other

No father, no mother, no sister, no brother

So until next time, if that is meant to be

My faithless love, when will you see?

JOURNEY'S END

2014

Has this journey come to an end?

In spite of all the love and faith I did send

The fear too deep for it to mend

Have I no coin left on you to spend?

I wish it not so, for to let you go

Means taking a new path with someone I've yet to know

The hurt, the loss, the confusion, the doubt

This was also what it was all about

Yet I learned to love in ways I ignored

And discovered all the emotion over the years I had stored

You opened my heart and made me feel

I discovered again, after many years, what it meant to be real

And though on this path you could walk but a mile

I knew your face when it wore a smile

When the fear was forgot

Our encounters so hot

To join with another

With neither to smother

The breath of life I breathed into your mouth

A warm wind of love, came up from the south

Carrying dreams which proved unreal

But while together, their strength I could feel

Nothing could stop me, my life was full

My heart knew one direction, towards you it did pull

These two plus years without you, a journey alone

First seeking out uncommitted sins, I would atone

Was it my fault, where was the wrong?

Why did the music go silent, no melody, no song?

I tried some anger thinking that might work

No longer an angel, just a jerk

No satisfaction came when love became hate

That was not to be our fate

So I worked my way through the thick woods of doubt

I sought the truth to find my way out

Of this forest of emotion, with no straight line of reason

Why is a pure heart so capable of treason?

I asked myself this question many times over

Felt its sear, yet I sought no cover

To find an answer, falsehoods must burn

And in time, with some luck, a page may turn

Revealing some answers, not the truth in whole

Drink the wisdom one can from the sacred bowl

Then continue the quest, look into many an eye

See the emptiness, hear their silent cry

For most ignore what they feel, put on a face

Stumble around, follow any path, any trace

With no thought of what is right or wrong

A rhythm they may sense, but not the song

No words, no meaning, no wonder, no lift

They walk in a daze, unaware, the forsaken gift

Of what might be if time and effort were given

If the trouble they took to heal their hearts, sadly riven

Around me I see mostly doubt and confusion

Ambivalence rules in this world of shifting illusion

What we know we build from experience, joy and pain

With each step, another piece of the puzzle we gain

Life is a task where we all must compete

To less noble matters it must take a back seat

This cannot be good, for to drive one must hold onto the wheel

And to know where to go, one must be brave enough to feel

Back to you now, I wonder, I care. How are you?

Have you returned to the old life or to something new?

I fear the former for that was your way

Your heart was silenced with no word left to say

Yet words aplenty fill your head

They are meant to distract, not inform, instead

For love is not for the faint of heart

It's a drama where each must play their part

Fulfilling a parent's legacy unwittingly passed on

Costumes given, not chosen, they unwittingly don

But we do have a voice, a will and a way

Where if we listen we can learn new lines to say

To change the course, find a path of our own

If we've paid the price and truly grown

This is what I have tried these two years to do

This journey of love lost has been at times a bitter brew

The hole in my stomach is no longer my friend

A broken heart found a way to mend

I miss you, perhaps I always will

But you alone may no longer be the only one who can fill

The muse, the source, the home my heart does seek

Though I've not seen the face, I am perhaps now ready for a peek.

I may fear a cost to this new door to open

That somehow I will lose the silent connection, too long still unspoken

Can a heart survive when cut free?

From its roots, blind and lost, it cannot see

In blindness one enters love's house convinced

That holy water has washed away darkness, eyes are rinsed

The visions we see hide as much as they reveal

They rob us of reason, logic they steal

So what is the difference, are we finally blind?

Is that the true nature of love in our kind?

Move forward in faith, life's essential fuel

Some say it's for wise men, others the fool

But without that hope, how to go ahead

Throw back the covers, get up out of bed

Face the now, whatever it brings

Pick up whatever instrument, stroke its strings

WHERE DOES IT GO?

November 27, 2012

Where does it go when love dies?

When the heart can no longer hide from the lies

Those told by each to the other

And those to oneself on behalf of another

A side of each one which fed the emotion

That filled the heart, as deep as an ocean

And like the turbulent seas green and dark

Hiding a truth, cruel and stark

For love is about completion, filling in the blanks

An armed division with holes in its ranks

Its strikes with force with little warning

The sun rises like some beautiful morning

We march into battle, heroes all

Unsuspecting that when it's over, both will fall

The battle is fought by phantom soldiers we imagine to be

In the eyes of the lover we think we see

And both play their parts, subjectivity in hand

Struggling to increase the foothold and claim more land

But once the day progresses beyond the noon hour

Shadows appear, then lengthen, things start to sour

What once looked like an unshakeable care

Starts to fray at the edges as both become more aware

That courage, so present, at the start

Doubt intercedes, as it comes apart

Each looks to their side, their tribe, their needs

Young shoots are pulled up, no one cares any longer for the unborn seeds

The ones lovingly set down on that first day

From the imagined truth, each starts to look away

Back towards from whence it came

Back to what it sought to first flee, such a perverse game

And so it plays out with each passing day

The once impossible question begins to gain sway

Shall I go, is this working, can it last another day?

Should I try, remain, believe or start to turn away?

Little thought is given to what might be lost

In saving oneself at the price of the other can carry a terrible cost

One's thoughts revolve, like some lonely orbe

Around oneself, to self-absorb

The world starts to shrink for others cease to matter

One's heart starts to shrivel instead of growing fatter

Content, safe, secure at first

But soon begins again, that initial thirst

The one that brought us to the well

From blindness into love we fell

The process repeats itself, we learn as we love

Each time to be different or the same, like some old glove

Wiser, if lucky, we take small steps ahead

Sampling along the way, we go from bed to bed

Yet what do we really learn of this central mystery

Do we write a new page or simply repeat history

If indeed we are like a military troop

With each member one strand in some complex loop

The gaps that exist, the ones we seek to fill

Are they seen in the eyes of the other, imagined until

We realize we have again fooled ourselves

Magical creatures sighted, gnomes, elves

Thrown back in the end to the land of no lies

The dust of battle settles, we see again with clear eyes

My strengths and my weaknesses define who I am

From this point alone can I make my stand

No easy answer exists, love can't transfer a trait

I alone can't open the gate

Complete me they can't, wish though I may

The real choice appears – do I run or do I stay?

The other is there to challenge and care

To see more with four eyes, new dimensions to dare

What do I want really once freed of these lies?

Can I find freedom from the past's heavy ties?

Stake out a claim to a life that is mine?

To mellow as I travel like some fine wine?

With you at my side, and me at yours

The truth, not the dream, was strong enough to open any and all doors.

But for this to become so, two must commit

The flame to burn long must be daily lit

That is the flaw in the world of today

My needs take precedence, they will have their say

To listen to them is a choice, not chemistry or fate

What we do will determine if we dine from a full or empty plate

CONFUSION

May 2, 2012

Confusion, that state of mind

When things seem unsettled, unfamiliar, unkind

It's a place where too many stay too long

Like a chorus too oft repeated of some popular song

But what is confusion? A permanent home?

One ultimately designed to keep one alone?

When life offers a chance to find what one seeks

Why is attraction followed by confusion after only a few weeks?

The answer oft given is "it's complicated," I'm confused

Is it me or the other or both who are being abused?

Confusion reflects a choice, a chance

To embrace life fully, or sit out the dance

So many excuses we offer ourselves

As we watch life go by sitting on the shelves

Of our fears and our hopes – we get caught in between

Some days the lights are red, others they turn green

But it seems as time moves forward, the days go by

The noises of pleasure give way to reluctant sighs

What to do for both sides tend to merge

Joy's song transforms into an inevitable dirge

Confusion is meant as a transitory state

How much should I eat? How do I feel about what's on my plate?

Am I hungry – of course – that is for sure

The first impulse provides the answer, simple and pure

But dare I believe, can I pull this off

Is the table set for me or do I feed at some communal trough

Thoughts and voices from the past grow with each passing day

The heart's yearnings are smothered, no longer to have their say

With each decision put off, delayed or ignored

Confusion gains ground, and the mind grows bored

For why want something if it is to be denied

And the reasons evoked, to myself I've lied

A vicious cycle of frustrated desire

The heart deflates like some punctured tire

If I do not stand and defend my needs

The past grows stronger, I get lost in the weeds

But is it by chance or an act of will?

It becomes easier with doubt my heart to fill

Not for me, but for others, or so it seems

Deluded in fantasy, they wander lost in their dreams

To believe what they say, only to recoil in the act

This is not some illusion, but a fateful fact

Embrace confusion, the faithless of heart

It provides comfort, excuses but most of all, keeps them safe and apart

So continue to believe in the mind's own tricks

Build your prison believing it a castle with these bricks

Cut the knot of confusion, some strings have no beginning nor end

When confusion endures, this is the message to send

INTUITION

September 12, 2012

As you know, when my thoughts turn to you

Something I've learned, something new

Perhaps not a milestone, but important nonetheless

As I, like you once said, long to progress

One of your last messages of explanation

When you speculated how I would recall our relation

You said you "….. were too immature to grow together"

And I refused – again – to fully understand, my eyes clouded by my inner weather

The storms raging within me at the thought of losing you

To be rational was something I could not then do

But in reflecting back, for you continue to live within me

There was another piece of the puzzle I came to see

As you frequently did, your intuition was just

My feelings prevented me. my judgement I could not trust

I rejected that thought, though you were right at a level more deep

All that mattered to me then was your heart to keep

Intuition is insight, coming before we can understand

It speaks the truth, but like walking on water, on it we cannot stand

I hated this thought, it smelled of defeat

That our hearts would no longer join, we would no longer meet

But in a way I'm sure you didn't truly know

You were telling me you weren't ready, for us together to grow

Too much road to travel still remains to be crossed

My efforts to convince you otherwise, did you feel like you were being bossed?

I hope you now know that this is not what I sought

And your efforts to tell me, through my own blindness and desire, came to close to naught

This I regret with all my heart

But all I did was to play my part

What choice did I have with my meager means

Emotions require at times dramatic scenes

In both our lives, our paths twice have crossed

And as long as I hold on to my love for you, all is not lost

For we meet in life, those we must

And all will work out smoothly, in this we trust

But life isn't like that, the road is tortured not straight

Of one thing I'm sure, what we shared could never be turned into hate

I entered your world to shake up your life

To make you feel new things, cut the tethers of the past with a surgical knife

Of seeds I've spoken often, to make you grow

For you can and must, for sure this I know

But time is the element, the irony supreme

Which we cannot control, which at present dashed our dreams

There are hurdles and challenges to be met

Before our true path can finally be set

For love to flourish at one precious moment in time

All the stars must come together and align

This rarely happens, for like our problems, they follow their own course

Before we met, they ran amuck like some wild horse

No direction clear, no purpose direct

To run, fear instinctive, the plains randomly to dissect

But love happens to set right things amiss

That's what I tasted so deeply in your kiss

But you have more in you, this I know

That is why these seeds were planted and must grow

It may take time, as your path you walk

Know that I watch (though not wait) for you from afar, though I do not stalk

I follow my own path, grateful for what you taught me

You showed me how to love and set my heart free

Ironic, cruel, wasteful and more

Why would life show us a way out and then slam the door?

But little matter, this is the way of things

For common man, princes and kings

These lines I write to let you know

That though different winds on our course may blow

I choose to believe that we will meet again

This is why there is no rest for my heart, nor my pen.

HELLO

Several weeks have passed

Since I wrote you last

The light went dim and I feared it lost

Something might have been gained, but with a cost

In my heart you remain

I see you more a bright spot than stain

Though reasons to want to forget would be many

To see only your faults, no qualities any

That would be wrong, denying what was

To blur a memory, evil does

Friends have asked me what I saw in you

Why did you touch me in ways fresh and new?

Answers abound though don't lead others to see

What I felt we shared, you and me

Words can convey only so much

To know the truth would require a physical touch

And though the hunger has passed

Something rich remains, a treasure that was meant to last

Empty now, though I continue to search

From lost soul and empty eye I lurch

Whenever I need something deep to feel

Whenever a closeness to my core becomes real

It's to you my thoughts turn, my cardinal point

How I would love your head once again to anoint

To shine a light and chase your dark

To walk with you once gain in the sunlight of the Park

Are you well, have you learned how to care?

Have you found your courage, are you able to dare?

As I have watched Novak* grow in strength

To watch him battle, go to any length

For that which he loves, though still now only a game

His quest is real, he is not lame

Not hobbled by fear, emotions run deep

From harm he is safe, always to keep

And should he win or should he lose

He will have learned that he is always free to choose

Winning can take so many forms with much to learn

That 's what makes the fire warm and bright to burn

So feel my care, hold it in your arms

Know I continue to cherish all of your charms

For though from others you hide the wonder of you

You showed it to me, your heart, oh too briefly, I knew

---

*Novak Djokovic, professional tennis player who came to represent the struggle to overcome one's self-limiting fears.

VALUES

PERSPECTIVE

May 2016

Son, Husband, Father now on my own

A westward wind brought me home

To start again where I was born

Thirty years spent in Europe, blinders away were torn

To see that different exists with as much certainty

Elsewhere, as here, monocular folly

Armed with perspective, things were seen for what they are

And learned to look beyond the near to see the far

On my return, though no doubt of from whence I came

My city, my country, its people – nothing was the same

Values, those things we cite as if our own

Guide our choices as if known

Yet when asked to name those we hold most dear

Incredulity first, then confusion, then fear

I should be able to speak of these pillars of truth

Together they're to guide me, the walls to my roof

I know I am right, never to question

Yet why when asked, all I encounter is indigestion

They tell me who to reject, though I can't say why

But most of all useful in telling me how to vote and what to buy

So what guides my feet as I navigate this land?

Why does it seem everyone's unhappy, yet can't take a constructive stand?

Something that lasts, bringing coherence and a direction clear

When I look too far down the road, all there is fear

In the years I was gone, so much change too place

Greed and selfishness became good, and upped the pace

Buzz words, tautologies, now became

And everyone started to think the same

As travel increased, knowledge of differences declined

Instead of opening up more, we grew more closed of mind

Fear will do that, if left to work unseen

Do what I want, but at all costs, keep my conscience clean

Blameless in the face of every failure or mistake

The fault lies elsewhere, for in fact, I've chosen to delegate

To some collective parent who preserves me from fault

Over serious reflection I now can vault

And if things go wrong, no thought to question my role

Even if wrong, my eyes stay fixed on the goal

But what is the endpoint I truly seek?

The one I believe will make me rich, strong and happy (God NO! - not weak)

Success is defined, like all else nowadays

In quantitative terms and monetary ways

Thus enshrined, selfishness and greed serenely rule

Not to learn but to network, that's why I go to school

What a waste of time, money and mind

We don't even see how we've become so unkind

Flat, superficial, devoid of depth and vision

Thinking is now the art of ridicule and derision

How will that lead us to a better place?

Survival is more than some frenetic race

How much is enough, for we live in a finite space

Limits are natural to teach us humility and grace

It's ironic, this quest for ever more

Do we realize what it means, what lies in store

At some point, as the past has taught

In our own net, inevitably we'll be caught

For if we always want more, what does that mean

Empty, we are, yet that remains unseen

And empty because there is a hole in the heart

What we put in leaks out, and we're back to the start

We are empty, so taught that what lies within

Is worthless, who would want it when rejected by kin

It's not that it doesn't exist, latent it lies

Starved of expression it lingers and dies

We eat with such knowledge, though no nourishment is found

The oceans dry up, the ship runs aground

Look inward across the emptiness that has become our own

Plant seeds of true connection, and watch by ignorant, insular winds be blown

Look far afield, yourself try and understand

The truth belongs to no country but between many a land

Differences are meant to distinguish, not part

Where certain are kept and others thrown out of the cart

The answer arises when perspectives blend

Wounds heal, rifts mend

And giving brings more than taking away

When in openness all have their say.

CONSEQUENCE

November 19, 2014

Consequence, a word no longer often seen

When words or acts spoken don't seem to mean

I stand by them, for they are me

Now they're lost, cast adrift, in a senseless sea

Was there indeed a time when I was defined?

By my words, like markers, left behind?

To trace my path – forward and back

Perhaps not a straight line, nor fallen into a bottomless crack

When did this happen? What made it so?

And what makes a person, and how are we to know?

Are we what we say, or what we do?

There was a time when together they lived, these twins, these two

But now, orphaned children, alone with no port

They can't grow up, rootless, daily they abort

Each attempt to mark their way, stone by stone

There is no longer a path, each one stands alone

To declare each day a new truth

No need for fact, no need for proof

It is what I say it is, for I am free to change

Funny how unknowingly, reality I rearrange

To suit my mood, my emotion, my fear

Who needs to see ahead, who values clear?

For consequence binds us in ways now lost

Our freedom comes now at too high a cost

Like ships adrift on a troubled sea

No astrolabe, no compass, no lighthouse, no tree

Bobbing each alone, colliding randomly with another

Who is this boat, a sister, a brother?

It matters little, these words too have lost their way

I can say the word, change their face, make them go or let them stay

For as long as it suits my humor of the present time

All power to me, it is I who define

Or so I may think, and for awhile it may be

But sooner or later on this senseless sea

Waves will rise, help I will need

No more water, no friend, no north star to heed

Then would I wish for something solid to know

To find refuge in this thing that stays – it does not go

Against time and the elements, it stands its ground

And I start to understand a truth I have found

My power, the illusion, drifts away like a mist

Leaving me lost, and helpless, at the empty sky shaking my fist

My way – no clue – where do I turn?

The light in the lighthouse – gone unfed – can no longer burn.

Who can I blame, since shameless I must always be

Why did not others take care, it wasn't my job to see?

Fingers point, voices in dismay and anger - all are raised

My omnipotence – so arrogant in times past – is no longer praised

Will I have learned, can I find my way?

Who will I listen to and what will the many thoughtless voices say?

If no one stands by the words they use

How can a future be built, how can we choose?

If nothing has been challenged, nor stood the test of time

Why take something seriously, believe in it, and make it mine?

If this then that, a simple construct

Proof in living, not a matter of luck

And so it goes, with my words and my acts

No fantasy, no magic, but reality and facts

Though these may change, as more we come to know

As all that we learn comes together, and we continue to grow

A foundation started from doing what we say

With brick and mortar, we build each day

And what makes it whole, allows it to stand

Building on bricks and not shifting sand

Is the proof I seek, the truths I test

Seeing what works least and what works best.

A word comes to mind from the beginning hence

To speak, to act, to live in consequence.

COURAGE

November 17, 2012

This word once spoken as part of a man

Defining his values, that for which he did stand

Rooted deep in his character, providing the glue

Directing him forward to things that were new

Other fears ruled the world in days gone by

Now we look at the ground when we walk, not the sky

What happened? What does this change portend?

Is it a beginning, or rather announcing an end?

What kind of message or prophecy does it send?

Are we that broken or can we mend?

What is this thing that made men strong?

That made them stand up and say yes, not afraid to be wrong

A brave-hearted "yes" swept the clouds away

Men didn't run from their hearts. They chose to stay

But we live now in a world where compromise rules

Where material survival and greed are the new crown jewels

No cause is worth the price, the chase

We pursue our tails in some pointless race

 Confused because no real values point the way

All that matters is that we can afford to pay

For that which appears to be worth the most

But the bigger picture, the long term, both may now be toast

Fear today rules the hearts of men

They no longer roam the land, but now live in a pen

Where any trace of the hero has been erased

No blood flows in their veins, only sticky white paste

Materialsim, so pervasive, fills their hearts

As they have forgotten their most important parts

It's just natural today to want ever more

The hero's quest is now fought in the mall, in the store

Banal. Trivial. Venal. Ordinary. Pointless

These are the new values replacing the once necessary "yes"

Robbed of their courage, the source of which they ignore

Has made cowards of us all, drained our hearts, made us poor

The consequences of this virus that's crept

Into our souls, made us prisoners, in some golden cage, like slaves to be kept

Free no longer to seek the path which is ours

We reside in McMansions, forgotten are the towers

That place on high from which to see far

No brave stallions to ride, only SUVS and crossover cars

I sound like some fool, some Mishima, enamored of a distant past

Praising partial truths in their original forms no longer meant to last

But some truth does remain in that which we've tossed

As we plod our way forward, ignoring the cost

In spite of our comfort, security and more

We've all become desperately poor.

No rousing lines, no words to inspire

Just give me a job and money - be a soul for hire

Disdain comes through my words, though this is not what I mean

A bitter lament is what I write, from what I've seen

When faced with a choice to see the unknown

To believe that this is what is meant to be grown

The seeds that are planted, that which is sown

No faith remains, no future is ours, it's only on loan

And so through our lives we walk timid and small

No faith remains that we can stand tall

Are we beaten by a world too big and strong?

By a place where we no longer feel we belong?

How long can we linger in a state such as this?

Does the lion roar or the serpent hiss?

The world has turned itself inside out

We've rendered ourselves sick with the gout

Answers are sought in a world outside

From ourselves we've discovered how to hide

FAITHLESS

April 12, 2012

This word one day came unexpectedly to me

In these times when politics mispeaks of spirituality

But I have felt a meaning deeper than this

Faithless means promises unkept, a treacherous kiss

I've told you of troubles with family forseen

These days filled with emotions harsh and mean

I challenge myself to find forward a way

But compromise, faithless, would be too high a price to pay

Words have meanings understood only in acts

With no consequence they are empty, no basis in facts

By all who have told me they loved me true

Unfaithful all, a motley crew

Mother. Father.   Sister. Wife. Lover.

From the searing truth there is no cover.

Better to see clearly that which is real

Treat the wounds and let them heal

But learn from this, not so ready to trust

Earned and proven, that is a must

Yet if applied as a principle, a rule

Keep one's distance, one's verve cool

Sort through the chaff, a seemingly endless line

Such a waste of our most precious time

If the bar is placed so high as this

What can be expected but another faithless kiss?

True it may seem, even feel real

Sit down at the feast, anticipate the meal

But until now, savor has lacked

The flavors of love placed in a vessel cracked

They've leaked from their store precious and rich

A tasteless meal, what a bitch.

Blended with care to create the required mood

No feast is found here, only fast food.

The recipe for which comes from fantasy fine

Imagined to a point of some aged wine

Impossible however, for the real to replace

In the hearts of those who know only haste

Love, and the meal that it is

Cannot be made quickly like some bubbly fizz.

Beneath the froth, substance is required

Without it union grows quickly tired

And so begins an endless round

Of silent new beginnings destined to run aground

Where is the courage, the care, the faith to make it work?

To seek out the light, no longer in the shadows to lurk

I pick myself up from each disillusion

Trying not to believe in the prevailing confusion

Where none have understood the why and the how

The fields will lie fallow, broken beside it, an ancient plow

The tool required to prepare the soil

For the seeds to grow and raise the blood to a boil

To unleash the passion dormant and still

If left unawakened, the future to kill

Darkness descends on these days obscuring the light

Strength seeps away, habit alone feeding the fight

Faithless race, unworthy, unfulfilled

At your own doorstep you will be billed.

Is there money enough in reserve?

The soul of us all to preserve

Or will we sink into our own morass

Of commoditization, amen, and all kiss ass.

For to treat our kind with so little care

Our spirits ground down through wear and tear

Fed only by greed and the self we indulge

Our hearts wither as our bellies bulge

Filled with air, emptied of worth

Death awaits us all, no more birth.

Is this the end or a new beginning?

Can redemption rise from too much sinning?

Does the pendulum swing to correct its ways

Or like the dead man on the gallows, does it foretell another end of days?

One which happens slowly, unannounced, unspoken

Can a people rise up once its spirit is broken?

Dark times await us, can we see our way through

Will the day be old or will it once again be new?

CHEMISTRY

October 13, 2012

Over these many months alone

I've sought a new place for my heart, a home

I've spent my love in places empty

And gazed in eyes for some look of plenty

Pushing onward in some vain hope

For that is what permitted me to cope

Nourishing the faith that what I found with you

I could find in another, and with them, my love, my life, renew

So far it has been a thankless task

No sunshine in my life like you, warming me, in which to bask

I close my eyes when songs I hear

Emotions rise and I sense you near

Faithless love, were you ever real?

Or was I only meant to discover again how to feel?

Imagining I could find you once again

Off I rush to find my pen

To write these lines, the pressure to relieve

And find the connection which allows me to believe

In you, in love, in the point of it all

To look at the sun, feel its warmth, stand once again tall

I wonder then how you survive

What is it that keeps you alive?

Has the darkness reversed for you life's way?

Abandon love so safe you can stay?

Differ we may, but deep inside

You revealed too much of your true self to hide

Touched each other we did in some special place

Though no longer here, there remains too strong a trace

So in spite of all I do to forget your face

In certain moments still my heart yearns for your love, your grace

Have I perhaps lost the sense of who you are?

Has my image of you strayed from reality too far?

From who you are, who you could be

Was it less about you and more about me?

I have no answer so the questions that remain

It comes and goes, bringing pleasure and pain

I sense perhaps I could crush this flame

Kill the feeling, give you all the blame

But something won't let me give up on you

And so the caring I feel rekindles anew.

Different now, no longer obsessed

Freer yet bound, still somewhere possessed.

Is this what love is about?

Should I resign, give in to doubt?

Yet without some friendly port of call

What is the point of it all?

Each heart that is born needs a home

So many travel, unaware, yet alone

Except in moments when darkness descends

And the illusion falters, the mask can no longer make amends

For the sins it allows, the lie to endure

With the sickness embraced, there is no cure

Yet each day they appear, iPhone at the ready

Devoid of depth or doubt, they seem so steady

Encounters occur, mostly random without point

With another illusion, their heads they anoint

The sacred oil not holy but tainted

Faithless sinners, unconscious, never sainted

What will it take to awaken from this slumber deep?

The heart thrives on promises it is meant to keep

But what if the language of love disappears?

What if emotions fall into arrears?

What if words lose their meaning , disconnected from acts?

What becomes of these sacred pacts?

The world comes apart, for the glue cannot seal

If lovers no longer know that which is fantasy from that which is real?

True it takes years to understand and know

That seeds planted take time and love to grow

Intent, a word not often used

Replaced by chemistry, a term inappropriate, abused

If chemistry is the new master of the heart

There can be no true beginnings, only a false start.

Chemistry exists but to attract

It was never designed as the foundation of a lifelong pact

Without intent to build, to see things through

Lovers come and go, passing through life, those we never really knew

We go through the motions, approximating some sense of what should be

Having no reference to clearly see

The difference between false and true

The sky remains clouded, never blue.

THREE MONKEYS

After many years spent in the fields

Planting and gathering what she granted to yield

Staying the line, thinking it right

Standing firm, the good fight

Rewards did come, and they were many

Though cumulatively speaking, little truth I found – hardly any

This species we are which we hold so high

Land, sky and sea, all waters we ply

Breaking the backs of those who resist

Signing on blindly, the dumb enlist

They hear other words, empty echoes from within

Unable to discern, grace from sin

Yet ebb and flow, forward and back

We stumble ahead, trying to track

Some phantom ideal that will make us great

When in fact what we do is overcompensate

The voices from within, there to balance our view

We ignore them willfully, never giving them their due

And so instead of give, we take

Rather than love, we nourish envy and hate

No simple equation in this dual world

Two flags, not one, simultaneously unfurled

How to choose, how to know

Which to follow, which will make us grow

Confusion reigns with no compass to guide

The path obscured, silence from the inside

For that is where truth in its ideal form

Takes shape, if we listen, where it is born

Unlike the three monkeys, who neither speak, hear nor see

The first, with senseless words, fills the void self-reassuringly

No sense does it make, for no thought comes first

Just noise, no exchange, a simple outburst

Unintelligible to others, and therefore ignored

Conversation degrades, all with it become bored

A single perspective counts, mine alone

I text, I tweet, I live by my fallaciously named smartphone

The second monkey sees, for that is how he moves

Reconstituting images in his own, as it him, behooves

Blindness results, for sight is a construct, always unclear

Come too close and all that results is fear

And what of the third, the one with hands on his ears

Do they keep the voices inside, and with them the tears?

Those shed when truth is smothered with intent

When the coin it should provide goes unspent

Experience is the currency our wisdom to buy

But all 3 monkeys need be free, though they must together ally

For truth too is a construct and hard to hold

Courage and care are required, we must be bold

Rather ignore life's lessons, preferring not to be told

So dumb, deaf and blind, a solitary path, we grow old.

But I must digress, the foundations are laid

What happened when the field for the forest, my way I made

As always illusions prevail, they lead us on

A new path, a mission, an idea, a new road to walk upon

One friend, then two, then three, then four

Each opened a bit more life's teaching door

Like a diamond in the rough, each one a new facet to polish

Too hopeful each time, my loneliness to abolish

A simple cut for me would suffice

If only I could trust, love and be allowed to be nice

But for reasons which still today evade my mind

No ready explanations, why they left, can I find

I've learned more of man and womankind

On words easily spoken I have often dined

But we are more what we do than what we say

This I've learned with pain, is humankind's way

TO DARE

June 11, 2012

To Dare

To Care

To try and be fair

To think of oneself alone or as half of a pair

To see oneself as part of something that's big

Without losing oneself like some fallen twig

Empty thoughts come from empty hearts

No voice, no muse, no inspiration, no charts

Where does this lead?

Are there warnings to heed?

Is there land in sight?

Or do we simply sail in some perpetual night?

Dark times have arrived, the sky fills with clouds

The world, it seems, has donned its shroud

Blind we all seem, no vision exists

Just anger emerging from the pits

Of primal emotion born of fear

As connections are lost with those who should be near

But this fear of which I speak

Derives not from a monster crawling out of some creek

One that we can see and know

One whose claws threaten some mortal blow

No the danger comes not from without but within

It is born of our greed, our selfishness, the names of our sin

When the us has passed leaving only the me

The land starts shrinking back into the cold sea

For stand we can on only the common ground that we build

Working together like members of some professional guild

With purpose, skill, hope and care

To tackle the difficult, the impossible, to dare

But "me" is weak, alone and unsure

The ills of its soul has no ready cure

So we bicker and fight amongst ourselves

We labor in disunion like demented elves

Dismantling that which we've built

Too narcissistic to ever consider any guilt

Blame the others, like children lost

Concerned only for themselves, regardless the cost

Does maturity have its antithesis

Is this, like some virus, what's truly amiss?

WATSON

Febraury 2016

Why is it that some seem to thrive?

And others, though equally endowed, struggle to survive?

We would prefer some neurological explanation

A quick fix, a pill, a shot, to cure the nation

As we pretend to understand more than we know

False wisdom, today's truth, the seeds of lies we sow

For no one really knows the answer to the fundamental question

Who are "we" beyond movement and digestion?

Some say the brain, the 3 pound miracle of fatty meat

No problem can resist its power to solve and defeat

Synapses, transmitters, receptors and all

We see pieces of a machine, without hearing the whole's call

Do I start out as a blank slate, as some have claimed?

Our culture, our parents, our environment - by them we are maimed

And arriving at some point – no one knows which it might be

The wiring is complete, a new being so defined are we.

But if that were so, should more similarities not prevail?

External differences aren't enough to make one a head and the other a tail

Somewhere along this journey, reductionism narrows our view

We see meat, potatoes, broth, vegetables, but none can describe the stew.

There are diseases, organic, tumors and the like

They change us in ways obvious robbing our voices, no substance, just a mike

Thank God we can fix some things, saving lives and our soul

Where once we were broken, we can become again whole

But there too, we look at the machine, its process and form

Thereby predicting some behavioral norm

This face we are called upon to present

Is hardly the sum of a life – no great house but a simple tent

What makes me myself, is the sum, not the parts,

This truth appears on no one's charts

 I own my house, I do not rent

How is my personality's capital to be spent?

And like a house, if built to endure

The foundations are laid solidly, safe and sure

For life is hard, adjustments must be made

And we learn more when we fall, wisdom must be paid.

There was a time when the brain seen as an organ of adaptation

Having no equal in adjusting to a new situation

Is that not intelligence, the ability to see order where there is none?

And find a way forward, survive, maybe even have fun.

Reduce me to synapses, deny me my soul

What inspiration does that provide me, what is the goal?

Perhaps the spirit weighs not 3 pounds, nor resides in my head

But without it I won't survive. I'd surely be dead.

When did we forget that things are always more than the sum of their parts

If we speak in metaphors, is that a reason to dismiss us and throw darts

To demean the truth so I can feign some advance

And those who struggle, does it really provide them with a chance.

To adapt means to question, oneself first of all

To open one's mind, watch chaos coalesce, hear its call

Search for answers, break things into ever smaller pieces

Publish useless data, claim progress, it's a business after all, press releases

More money for the obvious, give it a new name

Cast off past knowledge, start from scratch, that's the game.

What have we become, how have we gotten so lost?

Hungry for more data, who cares the cost?

The answer lies, too many believe, in Watson and its kind

Artificial intelligence is a myth, and not a mind.

The past a good predictor has never been of what's to come

Some feel it's all we have, if we can count something, at least we have a sum.

Philosophy, speculation, reflection, the use our mind

That's what has made us who we are, humankind

Do we feel betrayed by the ineffable, what we can't explain?

Or is it rather than if we can't control it, so we'd rather complain

Out with that which we cannot count

Hail the new God, at least a spreadsheet offer columns and an amount.

Are we unconsciously rushing towards the final delegation

When we've grown too lazy to govern ourselves, and abandon the nation

To some average ideal that doesn't exist

Thus to lose what's special, individual, the essence is missed.

Correlations are fine, they can point a way

Helpful, of course, they can digest data all day

No machine can create something meaningfully new

Bound by its logic, it's a sterile field where nothing grew

Intuition, fantasy, emotion, delight

Intelligence that's artificial should be welcomed without fright

Technology can replace man in his redundant task

Or follow instructions, if only we ask

But can it replace us in every way?

Only if we stop using our minds, AI may have its day.

If we see ourselves as only parts, not the whole

The essential is missed taking a terrible toll

For each one of us has possibilities to create and adapt to the world outside

Our true richness lies within, though from it we struggle to hide

No machine I can imagine a spirit or a soul may possess

Without them no true intelligence the immaterial, the ineffable can address.

THE CHEAT

August 6, 2014

Ever wonder how we really navigate our path?

As we move through vast oceans, we cut our swath

The choices we make, the turns we take

Who makes those decisions? Do we really understand what's at stake?

Perspective is something mentioned a lot

From point A to point B, our course we plot

But do we really see further and understand

If we're headed out to sea, or back home to land?

It seems to me from what I've lived and seen

Having some vague awareness of where we are, yet forgetting where we've been

Who can look back through the years and trace a line

From then to now across time

To my way of thinking it's the only way true

To see what we've learned and how little we knew

Surprised I'm sure the reaction would be

A line full of bends and turns we'd certainly see

What would we make of it? And in fact where would we be?

Would it look like a door without a key?

For the guiding force, the true North Star

Like the one in the heavens, lives from us very far.

And how often do we stop and look up at the sky?

How often do we stop and ask ourselves why?

What is the North Star, the one magnetic pole?

The one that draws us forward to make us whole

Is that really its purpose, the why it exists?

Or are we just fooling ourselves, one theory among many on one of our lists?

When we ponder our journey, seeking sense where there seems to be none

It can be dangerous, like playing with a loaded gun

How much light can our eyes bear, how harsh a truth can we see?

Even if that is the price to pay to set ourselves free

Why think such thoughts, too hard and impossible to know?

So let's not worry about what we'll reap and just continue to sow

But comes the dawn, out on our fields we gaze

Have we grown a garden or an impenetrable maze

For there comes a time in everyone's life

We are caught by our actions and have to deal with their strife

Of what we've created with no vision whole and complete

And realize the ignorance we chose amounts to little more than a cheat

LIFE'S NEW RULES

April 2016

When in middle age one's life comes unexpectedly undone

The parameters have changed, and so has the sum

We labor thinking the equation is the same

Yet all is different, and so is the game

Pick up the pieces, rebuild according to the old rules

And of course use the same tired old tools

False starts abound, we continue to believe

Unaware as yet how much has changed, ourselves we deceive.

The years pass, fruitless, older we've become

Suddenly it seems, we are under the gun

To reconstruct what no longer applies

A new innocence blinds us as we search for new ties

But in the time between then and now

We have understood the what, but not the how

To search for what was with someone better, someone new

Is it not like trying to revive an old stew

When a new dish, something we've yet to discover

Holds the key to finding a friend, a partner, a lover

Indeed, one must start anew

More blind than when young, and nary a clue

Old demons awaken, confusing the dance

Perseverance, that old friend, reduces the chance

To keep with the old ways, even if success they once did bring

The music has changed, and most are afraid to sing

Finally, I hope, a turn in the road

Failure can be a powerful goad

To let go, stop trying, turn the focus inside

When you've seen what's wrong, pointing it out won't turn the tide.

But how to let things happen when you've lived to mold your way?

To shape your world, your thoughts, and have your say

To let Life happen, is that the new direction?

When it has never been my predilection

How can it work if I don't lead the dance

Do I stand on the sidelines as if in some trance?

If we live in a world where opposites define

Logical it seems, if one approach fails, it must be a sign

Look to that which you haven't done

Take the foot off the pedal and let things run

For pushing each day brings its share of frustration

And drives our spirit to a darker nation

Look to the inside, create a void

If nature does indeed reject it, will she become annoyed?

And of her own volition, a remedy she sends

Then my eyes should be open to see when she makes amends

Not because some morality wants it so

But because that's how things at this stage of life are meant to go.

HOLDING PATTERN

September 2016

It's been almost 15 years since I came back

Hoping to set a new course, ride on a new track

Phase one, all things considered, was mostly a success

Though I now know for sure, I'd settled for less

But less of what, is more my due?

I kept moving forward, that's all that I knew

Believing that I could fix whatever went wrong

And for the most part, I made my place, felt I did belong.

Phase two was something of an intermediate time

Still young enough and supposedly wiser, I sought out what should be mine

Time flew by and I look at my years

Options seem to recede along with my fears

But one seems to grow, getting bigger as time passes by

A confidence in Life's generosity ages too, though I continue to try

Yet looking back it seems though wiser in many ways

The essential was missed along with the dwindling days.

What was I due? Is such an idea even real?

Children we remain, fairness itself rarely does reveal

When younger with a family, and the need to provide

I stuck to my course, and harder I tried

Like the cat with nine lives, though I never kept count

Vital balances like that we don't want to know the precise amount

Yet when I finally did hit the inevitable wall

When from HR I got the call

When it was only for myself that I had to see

Those 9 lives were gone, and it was only me

No solution came riding over the hill

No fertile field awaiting my till

Each initiative I took, in the end came to naught

I didn't know against which enemy I fought

So plodding along, deploying old methods tried and true

I managed each day hoping for some savior new

False starts too numerous to recall

Like some defective motor, life continued to stall

Yet here I am, wounded and scarred

And still in the game, I have yet to be barred

Lost many companions, precious and true

Though I fought with all I had and they were, in fact, but a few

With my 9 lives now gone, I look to this solitary road

To get out and keep trying, myself do I goad

Yet clearer with each setback hope no longer blind

Life can be cruel.   Life can be kind.

She cared for me when I needed her most

And for that I am grateful, lifting my glass in a thankful toast

But now that she's abandoned me, I received more than my due

The lots reflect random chance, if only I knew

For the rules have changed and the world as well

Flux becomes permanent, no one knows what to sell

Though products we've become in some grand market online

There is no truth any longer to structure our time

The future dissolves into some present without end

Why adhere to one's values if every rule must bend?

If that be the case and there are no rules, does the world then dissolve?

Is there any point to retaining one's own resolve?

Standing tall like some tree, resisting the wind's surge

Saying no when all others give in to every urge

No the world I can't save, who am I even to pretend?

If the fabric is riven, it's not mine to mend.

All I can do, or so it seems

Aside from looking inward for guidance and dreams

Is to focus once more on what I need to complete in this life

To live in some harmony, limit the strife

Without abandoning that which made me who I am

And continue to try to become all that I can.

A lonely road for sure, no companion in sight

Will I finish my days in the sun or the night

ALONE

June 2015

What does it mean to be alone?

Has one committed some sin for which we must atone?

If viewed from without, the perception is clear

There must be something wrong that others sense or fear

For why else would someone not choose me sooner than some other?

Don't they see my many qualities as father, son or brother?

I've lived in each space and tried my best

Did I somehow each time fail the test?

What other explanation could I find?

And if not, bring me someone or at least peace of mind.

There is truth in this, no doubt, we all have our ways

Why do some find and others remain solitary strays?

Who else could I blame, though fault always lies with others?

No matter who they be – friends, sisters, parents, brothers

But in truth, there is more than one rock to look under

For this is yet another of life's mysteries

Can the answer be found in reflecting on personal history?

But there again, it is back to me

Can any answer be found in my simple subjectivity?

Why does it seem there is no thee – only me?

For I live in a place full of others of my kind

And clearly, we are all not of one mind

Could there possibly be some validity in looking around?

In trying to read the lay of the land, study the ground?

For I walk amongst others, as they do with me

Are we all blind to ourselves, does no one see?

What is it that guides us all, what God do we truly serve?

Is it the one we talk about, or the one we deserve?

The one we have elevated by the choices we make

And the values thus incarnated in this world of take

How did this happen, and more importantly why?

When did we forget how to sing, recalling more surely how to cry?

Like some hungry baby, raging indiscriminately

Counting on someone, anyone, to take care of me.

Now pause for a moment, what does this imply?

Is there some truth here or just another lie?

Hunger comes from an emptiness within

It's a sensation, a hole, a pain, though not yet a sin

But the infant has no resources, no means to see to its needs

All it knows is the pain, the want, a thing outside itself on which to feed

"Take" makes sense in this particular case

Nothing wrong here, no hidden evil face

But as we grow, what do we learn?

We take what we want and the rest we spurn

Like being alone, there are two parts to this equation

Could the answer lie in some ailment plaguing our nation?

Hunger exists and not just for food

The first need of all is to belong to some brood

And if this need is left unanswered, if there's a hunger food cannot assuage?

What's left but a hole, a need and a deep seated rage?

If everyone takes, giving having been lost

Surely there must be a terrible cost.

So alone, or so the answer it seems

Needs no lengthy analysis of consciousness or dreams

If everyone is looking to take, never thinking to give

How can two people together possibly hope to live?

Of all the wisdom I've heard on this matter, where the truth has come to rest

Juliet to Romeo, said it simply, but best.

"The more I give, the more I have" her words innocently spoken

Heed them if from this nightmare you wish to be awoken.

HAVE WE ALL FORGOTTEN?

December 2014

Have we all forgotten?

Were we all misbegotten?

To be so completely lost

With no idea of the cost

That the heart no longer has a place

As life has become a blind race

To where and for what do we run?

And what do they mean? Joy, caring, fun?

The last remains, the operative word

I look up at the sky but see no bird

Bound to the earth, with no wings to fly

Vistas shrink when seen from the ground and not from on high

Left foot, right foot, repeatedly, we plod along

Only a vague recollection of the last popular song

The beat remains, the melody too, in part

But no words, no meaning, no point, no heart

Fill my head with senseless noise

No adults to be found, only girls and boys

Why grow up if no care I know?

Why build and struggle, why seed to sow?

If tomorrow brings only another today

And I find myself empty, with nothing real to say

Out of habit, or fear, or plain emptiness

I embrace no blame, pointing at others, never to confess

The role I played in this life I was given

I ran all the time, after something, I was driven

But put a name to it, see it from afar

It's shape hard to determine, a bank account, a vacation, a car?

No, it can't be that, those things come and go with increasing speed

Changing shape, and color, and price – driven by some mindless need

To have, to possess, to control and more

As if my pile of things my sense of self can restore

What binds us all, those many living here

Are emotions – these feelings all animals hold dear

But why should it be so, is a feeling just another expression?

When I've not explored its meaning, content to avoid all digression

I move on to the next thing – a word I choose with care

But to know its sense, its purpose, that I do not dare

And so I move on, no compass to guide my way

My heart silenced, I am not alone with nothing of interest to say

I look around, others appear to be normal

They are clothed, coiffed, moving in some pattern formal

Yet there too, where does it lead?

Is it feeding my soul, or making it bleed?

This is not me – it has never been so

Better than others? Perhaps, but I think no

I've felt from the earliest of times

Questions more frequent than nursery rhymes

Why live in a place, in a way, with others?

Who chose to ignore what binds us, sisters and brothers?

Family. Blood. Gender. Race.

We line up at the start, trying to keep up with the pace.

The speed increases over time, though the reason be unclear

It's the mob, the herd, stay close to avoid the fear

But step outside – at least from time to time

Consider the why's and wherefores, how I spend what's mine

If more questions arise than answers are found

Take note, your feet are now touching the ground

You can see a path starting to emerge ahead

A direction, a purpose, so much better to be alive than dead.

EVERYTHING RIGHT

January 2015

And what if I did almost everything right?

What if I followed the prescribed light?

What if I listened to all that was said?

And swallowed all the wise words that I've been fed

The values I was taught, to be strong and true

To believe that in the end the sky would be blue

That others of my kind would be of similar mind

That love and caring would lead me to find

That which is necessary to live this life

To be a good husband to a good wife

And in thoughtful caring my seed to sow

To be a good father and watch my children grow

In short, to shine my light and relish its' glow

To have done my best, this I know

To teach that which I believed to be true

To share with them all that I'd learned, that I knew

To speak the truth when asked what I thought

All of these homilies, values into which I bought

They were to lead me to a place, a home

A haven, a temple with a golden dome.

Has it worked out as I thought it would?

Have I found all that which I sought, done all that I could?

The answer should offer no surprise

Come up short, no gold ring, no great prize

Am I disappointed in the life that I've led?

Or do the questions confront me, what more remains to be said?

I've arrived in a place where in spite of it all

Illusions are harder to sustain, to hear their call

Most cling to the falsehoods they've spent their lives to build

Preferring their reality neither hot nor clear, but frosted over and chilled

Fear and disappointment have cost their souls

As dreams have shrunk and with them their goals

When I left this land of promise and hope

People believed they could do more than survive, than cope

But as wisdom has morphed into data points on a chart

What's been lost is that which resides in the heart

Quantify, plot, analyze numerically

With no thought or reflection, the new American folly

Lost perhaps as never before

Options dwindle, where is the door?

And if we found it, as some seem to believe

In returning to past ways, for days gone by they grieve

But not in some mournful, thoughtful way

No, full of anger and hate they have their say

Is this a way forward, together can we progress?

Or is it simply a matter of collective regress

As that which was built spins apart as rarely before

The whole explodes, including the core

That which held us together in the face of it all

Can ours, unlike so many others, survive the coming fall?

Or are we reaching some turning point?

Will another kingdom arise, a new head to anoint?

I fear for us all, in ways never discussed

Time shrinks, and so we too must

No longer to think thoughts great and high

All I want is more than my share of the pie

Will it satisfy me, will peace fill my heart?

Or will I wander further, dragging a loaded – yet too heavy cart?

For it's full of stuff, once thought worthwhile

If one has no substance, at least have some style

But without the former, one lives in two dimensions alone

That is a sin for which one cannot atone.

Look outward for answers – that's what I thought they'd said

What could I possibly find within, it's all dark, moist and dead?

But that's the point we've missed, the garden waiting to bloom

Fertile land therein lies, the only way to chase the gloom.

There I harvest what I have of worth

There all things find their birth

And thusly enriched, I have found what I always knew

That I kept alive as it grew

 If only I look, so much have I to give

And with that I realize, finally, why we live

THE HEART HAS EYES

December 10, 2013

The Heart has eyes, a thought perhaps quite new

In these times when we choose based solely on what we view

We assign to love, an all knowing truth

When times prove it wrong, where is the proof?

And emotion, its tool, its voice, its soul

Which strives above all else, with another, to make oneself whole.

So little thought is given these matters which chart our course

We bet our lives on what might be a blind and lame horse

But is this steed at fault, or does the blame reside within

Embraced ignorance, denying all facets of the unnamed sin

In our time when feelings shared are more fantasy than fact

When our subjectivity has reached such proportions we are blind when we act

We blame the other, for their faults are clear

Always safer to look beyond rather than see too near

Words oft spoken yet so misunderstood

We want to drive the car ignoring what lies beneath the hood

The motor of our movements in time and space

Has become less a reflective journey than some frenetic race

It's true, time is really to us all that's given

But like some unassailable wall, a stake has been driven

A cardinal point, the north star or how I feel

That's a place to start to find an even keel

Lacking a chance for a clearer view, a sense of self

We change partners, tossing one for another seen on some digital shelf

With this as the problem statement, the "why things don't work out"

The time has come to really ask, what's it all about?

Emotions, the word, yet surrounded with fear

In daily discourse, banalized, as if its meaning was clear

But ask another to explain its sense

Savant words will be offered in the present tense

Yet get too close and up goes the fence

And if you listen closely, it's all nonsense.

What if emotions are the thoughts and language of the heart?

How have we grown from them so far apart?

And why cling to things representing so little interest?

Isn't the heart just a big pump embedded in our chest?

So we deny these irksome intrusions which invade our lives

Inconvenient, mysterious, troubling, unavoidable, cutting at times, like knives

For they now imply a loss of control

And who really worries anymore about becoming whole?

Ignore them we may, run when we start to feel

With distance will the intensity fade, will I start to heal?

But am I sick? Is their presence the source of some disease?

Or is the real problem that when I feel, I feel ill at ease

Like someone speaking in a language I don't understand

An alien's tongue frightens. I don't see the outstretched hand

So further I turn from this inner truth

Preferring not a shared table but some isolated booth

When alone I control, to some small degree

What actually can transpire between you and me?

For the heart exists as the home of our deepest self

The place where who we are is stored on some living shelf

We learn to move on, not to dwell on the past

Never realizing that that is exactly where the die was cast

The cards we are dealt, and those picked up along the way

We struggle to learn how best them to play

Some are too painful to turn up their face

We fool ourselves into thinking they have no place

But what of the choices then, those we pick to love

Those who we believe fit us like no other, hand in glove

Only to discover in time they were not as we thought

And in that relationship, we feel trapped, we feel caught.

One thought - Never to return to the why's of our choice

We focus on their flaws, quashing our own voice

For we choose our lovers blindly for reasons pragmatic or not

Or as nowadays quite simply because we think they are hot

What an intemperate word, what does it truly mean?

It speaks of fantasy, a glimpse of who we wished we had ourselves been

For like the ancient peoples of old

Who when having conquered an admired foe, courageous and bold

Would his heart eat, for qualities they wished they had

This metaphorical completion reflects something quite sad

It speaks to one's own sense of inadequacy

And that need for wholeness, is based purely on what one can see.

But the deeper truth, the one which could guide

Is now lost, no time to waste, from what it might tell me. Most prefer to hide.

FAITHLESS

April 12, 2012

This word one day came unexpectedly to me

In these times when politics mispeaks of spirituality

But I have felt a meaning deeper than this

Faithless means promises unkept, a treacherous kiss.

I've told you of troubles with family forseen

These days filled with emotions harsh and mean

I challenge myself to find forward a way

But compromise, faithless, would be too high a price to pay.

Words have meanings understood only in acts

With no consequence they are empty, no basis in fact

By all who have told me they loved me true

Unfaithful all, a motley crew

Mother. Father.   Sister. Lover.

From the searing truth there is no cover.

Better to see clearly that which is real

Treat the wounds and let them heal

But learn from this, not so ready to trust

Earned and proven, that is a must

Yet if applied as a principle, a rule

Keep one's distance, one's verve cool

Sort through the chaff, a seemingly endless line

Such a waste of our most precious time.

If the bar is placed so high as this

What can be expected but another faithless kiss?

True it may seem, even feel real

Sit down at the feast, anticipate the meal

But until now, savor has lacked

The flavors of love placed in a vessel cracked

They've leaked from their store precious and rich

A tasteless meal, what a bitch

Blended with care to create the required mood

No feast is found here, only fast food.

The recipe for which comes from fantasy fine

Imagined to a point of some aged wine

Impossible however, for the real to replace

In the hearts of those who know only haste

Love, and the meal that it is

Cannot be made quickly like some bubbly fizz.

Beneath the foam substance is required

Without it union becomes quickly tired

And so begins an endless round

Of silent new beginnings destined to run aground.

Where is the courage, the care, the faith to make it work?

To seek out the light, no longer in the shadows to lurk

I pick myself up from each disillusion

Trying not to believe in the prevailing confusion

Where none have understood the why and the how

The field will lie empty, and broken beside it, an ancient plough

The tool required to prepare the soil

For the seeds to grow and raise the blood to a boil

To unleash the passion dormant and still

If left unawakened, the future to kill.

Darkness descends on these days obscuring the light

Strength seeps away, habit alone feeds the fight

Faithless race, unworthy, unfulfilled

At your own doorstep you will be billed.

Is there money enough in reserve?

The soul of us all to preserve

Or will we sink into our own morass

Of commoditization, amen, and all kiss ass.

For to treat our kind with so little care

Our spirits ground down through wear and tear

Fed only by greed and the self we indulge

Our hearts wither as our bellies bulge

Filled with air, emptied of worth

Death awaits us all, no more birth.

Is this the end or a new beginning?

Can redemption rise from too much sinning?

Does the pendulum swing to correct its ways

Or does it foretell of another end of days?

One which happens slowly, unannounced, unspoken

Can a people rise up once its spirit is broken?

Dark times await us, can we see our way through

Will the day be old or will it once again be new?

THE PATH TO MY POWER

June 2016

When I was a young man, searching for my power

I wondered where it would take me and when would be my hour

No help from a father, absent, not there

Who would show me the way if he did not care?

What shape would it take and what role was I to play?

Bigger. Stronger. Taller. Smarter – in none of these could I have my say

So I landed on wisdom, this inner source, invisible yet strong

This was to be my journey, to myself I would belong.

I would look inside, to the depths of my soul

I would pay the price and thus fill my bowl

Owing nothing to anyone, none could take what was not given

And on my way, quietly driven.

The past weighed heavily, a new venue I sought

In this foreign land, I laid down the stone, my freedom was bought

Amazing how liberating life can be

When surrounded by new eyes one's past does not see

No constant reminder of other's perceptions

Nourish they do self-fulfilling deceptions.

So student, boyfriend, husband, father and more

Life took shape before me, with images of what might lie in store.

Those early years were full, responsibilities making of me a man

An image of what that meant took shape - it was all that I can

Thus guided from within, life's travails shrunk to a manageable size

Innocent I was to the real dangers, I came soon to realize.

Spouses are guided by missions of their own

Some seek to grow, others wish only to clone

Lies are told, compromises are made

Loyalty guided my conduct, and so I stayed.

Each role fulfilled added a new dimension

What was missing before, now complete convention

I was Father, Husband and provider

There were no caveats, exceptions, no rider.

One can heal oneself, it's a choice one makes

Some believe it possible, others prefer their same mistakes

With each task completed, the children now on their own

I look on with love and pride at how they've grown.

But now arrives a challenge unexpected

What to do with this heart with none elected?

To share in whatever of care I have to give

This last great adventure I have to live.

If one's own heart is full, it yearns to shine

To shower in warmth the one who would be mine

And likewise to watch the other prosper and grow

And learn and listen and come to know.

Wisdom is bought with experience, there is no other way

We take a stand and have our say

We listen and learn, to share when order we find

To care for the other, evolving in body and mind.

So what has my journey taught me of wisdom, this path I took

That its power resides in understanding, there is no recipe or book

No power to alter the course of events

To look at chaos and find some purpose, so it makes some sense.

Disappointed? The child perhaps had hoped for more

To be as big and as strong as that boy next door

But the depth and the peace that comes to the curious mind

To know that life is a river – sometimes cruel, sometimes kind.

It's how we embrace what is given, the source of real strength

To care enough to go to any length

To embrace what is offered and bear the rest

That is wisdom. That is the test.

LANGUAGE AND WORDS

September 2016

> Language and words are the implements of thought
>
> They permit awareness, as to use them we are taught
>
> And from simple utterances expressing immediate states
>
> They grow so in power, expression and tastes.
>
>
> With them there is nothing we cannot express
>
> They allow us to make sense when all else seems a mess
>
> Yet do we respect them, individuals all?
>
> Focused and sharp in their meaning, can they answer the call?
>
>
> They blend together in dissonance and rhyme
>
> Building with them we can move in and out of time
>
> For only words survive – whatever their form
>
> They allow us to live together, making clear the norm.
>
>
> And even then, no tyranny do they impose
>
> Some truth emerges from conflict as their meaning grows
>
> They reflect more than style, culture or erudition

They define our souls, our civilization, our tradition.

Whether spoken or written, what else survives?

No matter the weapons used, guns, gas or knives

Yet in today's world where we proclaim the need to communicate

Technology providing the means, but in substance, how do we rate?

Listen to your neighbors, how they speak

Are words respected or havoc on them do we wreak?

Deforming their shape, their sound, their soul

Have we not mangled them, making them less whole?

Colloquial is fine as a condiment, adding spice to discourse, to make a point

But if you think about it, what comes to mind when one says place or joint?

For some they are interchangeably used

Until such time as both are abused

And in the moment, their clarity recedes

No longer is there a lawn, but only weeds.

For thought to be useful, precision is required

Conventions exist so in confusion we do not become mired

And with this precision in the use of words and thought

Rigor, a method, a standard to the process is brought

To sharpen in clarity that which is experienced indirectly

For what we represent with words is reconstructed subjectively.

Without these implements to which we give nary a thought

Human civilization emerged from the swamp; freedom was bought

Now what might happen if forces centripetal take hold?

Making it original and chic, deconstruction bold

Without wishing a linguistic nazi to be

Only with our words and thoughts can into the future we see

If everything slides towards what's loosely called "individuality"

What my friends is to become of the collectivity?

For it is the us – not the me – that has made us who we are

Marshalling our forces, we have indeed come far

And should we somehow find a way

To forget for a moment during the day

That I am but a small cog in a universal machine

And if it's each man for himself, can I help but become mean?

For without cooperation, the necessities of life

Can only be procured through conflict and strife.

Reflection, a seemingly dying art

Is that infinite place to imagine, completely apart

From the usual constraints of money and time

Hearing new insights, ideas that were not mine

Immaterial, yet real, solutions therein take form

Problems dissolve as answers are born.

So when facing another and we appear to talk

If neither is listening and we both seem to balk

Ask yourself what the reason for this might be

What prevents a common ground to emerge from the boiling sea?

Am I expressing something universal in words both can seize?

Or am I just making noise, shooting the breeze?

Common, a word nowadays much maligned

With originality all things must be signed

Are we lost in a world now of subjectivity?

Where the very thing which can save us is sacrificed to one's personal proclivity?

Common can also suggest universal, that which can unite

And just perhaps, point us away from the darkness and towards the light.

EVIL AND GOOD

July 2015

We speak often of the role in this world of evil and good

Institutions proclaim their truth as if they understood

Good came first, or so they say

But no one can explain if this is so or why it must be this way

From our perspective, small as we are

Our view is limited, we can't see very far

Now if the idea of evil having come first

Our neatly organized safe bubble would surely burst

The wonder of creation most certainly derives

From some ultimate goodness that all else survives.

Look around you – both far and near

What do you see mostly – strife and fear?

Where is the harmony, the peace spoken of?

Where is the blue sky and the white dove?

My observations have led me to start from a clean slate

What has driven humanity more – love or hate?

And what if hate came first, division and strife

How can we make sense of existence and life?

If indeed evil came first and chaos ruled

Something had to be done, our species needed to be schooled

The Devil sat on his throne, not God divine

For some savior, no doubt, we all did pine.

So God was invented, an alternative view

It was a bold idea, inspiring transformation and most of all, new

Now if God didn't throw the Devil from heaven, cast him to Hell

Perhaps it's the opposite, since goodness is the harder sell

It calls upon reflection, seeing beyond one's desires and needs

Understanding that giving is more nourishing, another's heart it feeds

And what is new must struggle, its place to create

Evil held all the room, good arriving late.

And how could it push evil aside?

Offering values and rules by which we need abide

Good isn't a fact, more an ideal, to inspire

To step into cool soothing waters and put out of the fire

To imagine a place where violence and hate do not rule

And serving my better needs doesn't make me a fool.

So if the Devil sits in heaven on high

Watching with pleasure as we carve up the pie

Obeying his rules of greed, envy and lust

Live for today, for tomorrow will surely be a bust

Against the immediacy of serving base desires

What can be offered, what inspires?

So I close my eyes, imagine a special place

Where harmony reigns, and life is lived not as a competitive race

Institutions we build, surrounded by improbable tales

In opposition to evil, good stands alone when all else fails.

No allies, no friends, no support to rally hence

No defensive walls, no towers, nor feeble fence

We look to the sky – like a screen on which to project a dream

The image, insubstantial, nothing but protons in a beam.

So is Goodness nothing more than man's attempt?

To put some order in this violent world so unkempt?

Yet when God's tenuous hold on our souls is shaken by events dire

We cast off our cloak of Goodness and leap back into the fire

And so it seems to go, this story of Man

We dream of a better world but rarely do all that we can

Not some Pollyanna fantasy, saving each day the Earth

But seeing joy in creation, with each new birth

And understanding Death is not evil, he takes back what was always his perhaps

Does that reduce tragedy to simple mishaps?

Our narrow view of life turns dark, and its taste sours

Is that too one of his essential powers?

Is there an answer, a way to look at it all?

Is there some way to rise above and not fall?

Our imperfections, our dark beginnings will they haunt us forever?

Like evil, they came first, those roots we cannot sever

But this is a place to plant, though dark, the soil is rich

If when challenged we consider, and don't just twitch

Though consciousness resides within me, I am not all

If I learn to care more widely and against darkness stand tall

To look from above the clouds, and see beyond my nose

And put things in their true order, to know the source from which all flows.

Evil came first, that we cannot change

We can dress it up, and try to rearrange

But the truth will resist, it can't be what it's not

Cold is cold – that's a fact – and hot is hot

But we can step from the swamp, though we will always smell

And listen to the wind, and hear the bell

The one that calls us to be more than we are

To look beyond our walls, to see far

To know what is good, to recognize it's feel

That's how good will prevail, and may someday become – like evil - real.

TURNING BACK TIME

December 2016

Is it possible to be born in the wrong time

When what seems obvious, worthwhile, benign

When caring and connection are more than just words

Only to discover they've flown away, like migrating birds

To another place, a land unseen

Perhaps to escape the harsh, the empty, the mean

To sow the seeds of a beginning fresh and new

That one day such a world will be for many and not just a few.

But that time is not now, the time where we live

Is more about take, forgetting what it means to give

The equation looks more like an invoice or bill of sale

How else could it end?   It can only fail.

As the spending dries up, we've bought more than we need

Though the hunger remains, its motor is greed.

Slowly, over time, the reasons we knew

Have withered away as the dry winds blew

The institutions on which we've proudly stood

Now disappoint us, as if we understood

Why they were meant to endure over the years

To protect us from ourselves, from our fears.

We recoil before the prospect of the changes unwittingly wrought

And blame anyone but ourselves, that's how we were taught

When faced with the unknown, rather than learn

We spin apart, on each other we turn

Seeking certainty where there is none, that's not what life's about

Like children we look for saviors, swallowing their lies so stout.

"Promise me the world and I'll follow your lead"

With no thought as to consequences, why warnings should we heed?

Can we really return to a past that exists in myth and memory alone?

Does that not also imply we abandon all the ways that we've grown?

To be great again, what does that mean?

It's a statement of defeat, of the frightened has been.

There is but one direction that life does know

Spring returns each year – but different – and things that way grow

Never two years the same, that's Nature's way

Avoiding stagnation, and the price of denying change, always too high to pay

Look to a future unformed, to be molded each day

Its promise is fulfilled only if together we stay.

Hope is born of courage, not from fear

So look to the horizon and not into your glass of beer.

To forget your woes, to nourish your hate

It may fill you up, but empties your plate.

It's hard, I know, to dream when the tide recedes

When good news is scarce and the bank account bleeds

But there was also a time when the waters flowed

When we chased a better life and the sun glowed

What changed our course came not from outside

The truth from ourselves we must no longer hide.

No conspiracy, no evil, no "other" of lesser worth

Made our future shrink in length and girth

It was ourselves, feasting and drunk on how wonderful we are

Look at my house, my tv, my iphone, my car

Fat, selfish, we did it all by ourselves

Are you kidding me? Are you some kind of magician, wizard or bunch of elves?

We sink or we swim together, the common good

That's the real motor, what lies under the hood.

Ignore it and what's happened could not have been otherwise

The way forward is not backward, there can be no other solution to devise

Believe the lies at the peril of us all

Think differently from before or beware the fall.

INNOCENCE

January 2014

I've walked on the edge

When the day grew dark

When life lost its promise

And the prospects looked stark

I sought salvation in wrong places, myself to forget

Empty pleasures proved to be a losing bet

When the answer to misery was to pile more on

No new clothes, just a shadowy cloak to don.

Indulgences provided solace for a time

They worked for as long as the illusions were mine

But fantasy dissipates, like exhaled smoke

What once looked good, now just looks broke

Insist we may, always knocking on the same door

Believing that what didn't work once, could work, if we only tried it once more

Until finally, the pool runs dry

And all that's left is an empty sky.

When the truth emerges, like the sun from behind a hill

The emptiness appears for what it is, with substance we need to refill

But what is this thing that allows to renew?

Does it come in liquid form, like some magical brew?

Drink may quench a parched throat

But it cannot carry me to the other shore; it is not a boat.

And what of the flesh, which promises so much

A cure can seem to come from another's touch

But for that cure to last, a renewal must be real

Something much deeper must be found, one has to feel

Feel what, one might ask, to begin again

A twelve step program, eleven, maybe ten?

Look back to what defined us, what we lost on our way

What gets stripped from our souls, bit by bit, each difficult day

What seems to only diminish with time, never growing back

Like a once smooth new wall, now marked by a deep crack

If character is seen by the lines that mark our face

Life's hardships indeed have left their trace

No, it's not our wounds which make us strong

Which point us home, time and again, to where we belong

It's the primal pool from which we originally came

Do you remember? What was its name?

What is always fresh and always new?

What believes in all that we can do?

What erases times cruel strokes?

And makes us forget how we were broke

What do we think once lost can never be again found?

What can lift the boat when its run aground?

Innocence, that which we speak of as lost

As if it were the price of entry, life's buy-in cost

But what if once again, it could be found?

What if through sincerity we could once more hear its sound?

The sweet noise of Spring on an April day

When Nature speaks of new life, with only new words to say

It is part of life's cycle, to offer another chance

Do we look it in the eye or cast but a fleeting glance?

To emerge from the darkness we must drink its fill

And if we are real, the toxins it will kill

Not our soul, but like some magical drink

The child inside feels again, and forgets to think.

Of all the reasons why things must be such

Why we have so little when our hearts crave for so much

Settle we're taught, let go of our heart

Live life in disconnected pieces, keep them apart

For to make them whole, to let them see

The purity of you, the purity of me.

Words like these we've vanished away

We no longer hear them say

"Bathe in your innocence, the waters from which you came

Open your heart, claim a new name

The one that was yours on the day you were born"

Like a baby's hair, before it was ever shorn.

Innocence can grow back, it's happened to me

When my heart was open and I'd found a "thee"

For love alone, can work its magic this way

From the incantation, these words its must say

And out from the darkness to walk away

And begin refreshed the longed for new day.

THE UNLOVED

THE DECK

March 25, 2014

Though the cards you were dealt, on the whole, were unfair

And they led you to believe that no one would ever care

Into the darkness you could only stare

As your options shrank, believing no more you could ever dare

To have anything you wanted in this world you did choose

Hope disappeared, believing you could only lose.

You broke my heart with your story of the unswallowed load

You came to think of yourself, no prince, but a toad

Perspective was lost on the good cards, your hand

And your future began to sink into the sand

But you showed me more than you let yourself see

And I tried to send back the image of all I know you could be

To do that, however, implied such a huge change

It could only frighten, discourage, derange

Perhaps I went about it in the wrong way

I know only to speak my heart and have my say

Did you think by speaking to you as I did

I spoke like a father to a kid?

That I thought less of you, withdrawing my care

Causing you to add me to your list of those many unfair?

Or did you fear to hope for more?

That if you dared, slammed shut yet again, would come the door

So better your losses early to cut

And return, defeated but "safe" back in your rut.

Times there were when frustrated I felt

When you could not free yourself, loosen your belt

For I too have needs, wants and desires

They burn within me, at times raging fires

Reason interprets the flames as best it can

Never sure if your fires they will dampen or fan

Reason tells me move on, I should

I've done it before, so I know that I could

But I saw in you too much promise and good

And so chip away at your walls, my ground I've stood

Perhaps I can't help you embrace the change you sought

When you came to me not sure of in what you were caught

But the prison is not the one you feared with me

It's the one in which you hide, you flee

I showed you myself for I wanted you to see

A direction, a purpose, a way forward to be

Not a copy, nor a clone, nor any such thing

But a chance to speak, to grow, to sing.

You have music within you – one of the good cards you were dealt

It's been hidden, ignored, ill-considered, unfelt

That's what I saw, what you showed of yourself to me

And even now, through your silence, I refuse not to see

I will not think ill of you, for that's not who you are

I continue to believe that you can go far

Success is promised to no one at first

How far they go depends much on their thirst

Risk inhabits this world we didn't choose

But we can also win if we try, not only lose.

I can't promise a future myself I don't know

But I can promise a friendship which if allowed, will continue to grow

And loyalty, in your corner to stay

Until the end of the road, the final day

Can you do as much, my friend to be?

Or is it too much responsibility?

Can you fight for another when they can do no more?

Or when asked to help, do you look for the door?

For another can you be stronger than for you alone?

Or there too, does your courage weigh you down like some heavy stone?

Is that what scared you when I said to you I would look

In time of need, when I sought a friend, not a crook

Someone who would give and not just take

Who felt in our friendship they held a stake?

Many thoughts and questions I've raised – my usual fare

You know me well, it's because I dare to care

Yes, it requires courage to want, to hope

But without them we don't really live, just cope

So once again, reach out to you, I know you are there

What you will do, come back to me or remain in your lair?

Only half the equation is truly mine

Play my cards my way in my own time

As you will do the same with yours

Will they open or remain closed – these doors?

But remember one thing, constant and true

It was obvious, something I already kne

Time is all we really have, it ticks away

And we waste so much of it each and every day

Seize what you have, forge ahead

Better to be alive than inside dead.

You are good. You are smart. Somehow you've learned how to care

Now all that's lacking to move forward is the will to dare.

As we grow in life

And face its inevitable strife

We seek to understand

That much is wrong and we all need a hand

To find a path to new ground, a new land

There to try again, and make our stand.

How often do we resolve that things must change

That the past must be lost, a new life to rearrange

We start out small with goals in mind

Looking forward as if that's all that's needed for us to find

Yet how did we get here, where we are?

Have we progressed little, or have we come far

And from where did we start, what pointed the way?

What guiding light in our lives has held sway?

Surely our parents set us on a path

Having steeped us in the families' too often toxic bath

Of turgid waters, conflicts spanning generations

Unconscious yet operative, driving our sensations

If we look back, the road traveled we see

It's the road ahead which forks that will define who we'll be

One path continues from what we received

If followed the outcome from afar can be perceived

And what of the other, the one less taken?

Why do we shy from it, preferring to sleep than awaken?

Change is a word full of promise and hope

Yet we fear it above all, for we must let go of the rope

The one that secures us so we won't fall

Is also the one that binds us, so we can't stand tall

In each one's life there comes at least one point

When we have a chance to change and leave the joint

To see ourselves with eyes freed from the past

And taste of our freedom, for real, at last.

We approach this fork with verve and more

As it comes into view, we begin to sense what's in store

The taste of all the good things that await

Once we cross the threshold and open the gate

We touch the handle, push it down

Swing it open, and suddenly a frown

Replaces the smile, the confidence, the hope

Something pulls us back, wait it's that rope

The final step, the one that will set us free

Night descends and the other side's promise we no longer see

Something has replaced that which drew us near

Its faceless aspect we can't describe, but we recognize it.....it's fear.

He – or she – who lurks below

Waiting for the moment to strike the fatal blow

To pull the plug, snuff out the light

Filling our hearts with every fright

Every fear we've met on our way

Even the ones from our earliest day.

And together they strike, each in succession as required

Until the fire which called us forward has expired.

We turn away, look back and no longer ahead

The unknown future suddenly fills with dread

And so we cling to from whence we came

We may call it something else, but it still carries the same name.

The past was written by another's hand

It carried briefly illusions of some promised land

But to enter this place where all is unknown

Where none of the old crops have ever been sown

Where familiarity ceases to exist

My hand now empowered, I can make a fist.

I can forge a new future and call it mine

Step out of the timeless, and plant a sign

This life belongs to me, I have made it so

I will decide when and where I will go

Courage fills my heart and makes me strong

I hear the music, I sing my song.

But wait, what's happened, I look around

This place looks familiar, I hear oft repeated sounds

Calling me back to a time when I was not free

To a time when I let others define me

A decision point, a moment of doubt

Is this new land a place of plenty, or one of perpetual drought?

Indecision takes hold, stops me in my tracks

I turn my head around and start to look back

Can I? Dare I? What awaits?

What's on the other side of the gate?

Was it all fantasy, illusion and dreams?

Was it hot air that filled me to burst at the seams?

Others have told me I was a certain way

A thousand times this I've heard them say

Rarely directly with no ill intent

The result was there, they said what they meant.

Each generation sends two messages strange

One of inertia, the other of change

Go forward, be yourself, take hold of your life

Fear not the struggle, the conflict, the strife

But whispered in tones barely audible to hear

The message is unmistakably clear

Don't do it for I rule, my name is Fear.

I REMEMBER THE CHILD

July 7, 2014

I remember the child – perhaps the first image I see

A small boy in his bed, on his left soft toys aplenty

They were many of all different breeds

Perhaps each different one addressed a particular need.

But those distant days are too far away

In his mind these were his friends with whom he did play

The care that he gave them, seeing to their every need

Feeling each one's character, giving them all his love in thought and deed.

Bedtime was always the busiest part of the day

Piled high on his left, covered carefully, there they would stay

Until the morning came, for sun always seemed to fill the room

When you're that young, the hours mean nothing be it midnight or noon

Other memories resurface, the next stage came

These friends would get hurt, he was their doctor in everything but name

Tend to their wounds imagined yet to him real

 He put bandages made of gauze, better to make them heal

 Recover they did, for most stayed many a year

Never alone was he, so he knew no fear.

Later came a time when this caring for others took hold

Mostly in his mind, for he was not that bold

A dancer he'd seen at his sister's lesson from afar

As she shone amongst her young peers, she worked at the bar

Her ankle, he thought, was broken somehow

Her pain left untreated, this he could not allow

And so in his world of imaginary healing

Where the most important was to open his heart, his feeling

For this was the source of his strength, whatever power he would find

To treat others with caring, and be gentle, giving and kind

But life isn't fair and favors none in this way

Impartial, uncaring, distant her way

Let happen what will, look on in neutrality

And barely take note, for what will be will be.

We choose not at first how to look out of ourselves

Our views are limited, simple people, not magical elves

 Events take hold, challenge us every day

Step by step, prodded we make our way.

 A cost is paid, though not in coin or bill

We take from our essence, and drop it into a bottomless till

Unaware at the time of what has been lost

Nor even taking notice how high was – or will be - the cost

And as self-awareness grows and issues take shape

The gaps from these levies are bridged by psychological tape

The whole that we were born to grow into and become

Has been broken into pieces, adding up to a lesser sum.

So we keep it together, noting the gaps and the holes

Fearing them, we shield our eyes from the light of their truth like moles

This puzzle, broken, incoherent, misunderstood, incomplete

Facing each day through it is no small feat.

Most accept that this scramble is who we really are

And sit behind the wheel, content to drive this fractured car

If the damage isn't too bad and the tape does hold

We can make our way in life, until we get old (believing we're safe from the cold).

But the harm that is done, to ourselves deep in our soul

Has consequences greater for the larger whole

For if we see the world the same way ourselves we understand

What of the others – do they too live in this broken land?

And if all perspective is deformed, our vision untrue

A new purpose emerges, one never spoken of, yet providing the glue

To keep the pieces somehow sticking together

Whatever life throws our way, whatever the weather.

But if the compass is broken, or worse intentionally misread

And the knowledge thus derived tells us lies, and we are misled

Not by some other, to whom we assign the blame

It's the mirror with no reflection, for our's is the name

The one who chose this bad compromise

Signing the contract with distortion and lies

To lift up the rock to see what lies thereunder

Would split the heavens, rock our world with thunder.

The demons we banished to the forgotten corners of our mind

Have grown powerful in the darkness, bonding with others of their kind

The more we ignore them, the darker their anger does grow

To frighten us ever more, for every weakness they know.

But the sun shining on the moist soil under the rock

Dries up the mess, and we can begin to take stock

What looked so foreign, so unlike us in every way

Its aspect changes, we start to hear what it has always tried to say.

For if of ourselves that's all we've come to know

If we planted in mud, and nothing did grow

And what remains of the time we've here spent

Nothing was ever bought – we always did rent.

When the circle closes and the battles are done

Night descends, and with it, so disappears the sun.

DISTANT CALLS

December 2015

I met a young man the other day

Intelligent, even charming, yet with too much to say

Why so many words to explain his state?

Clearly a mess was piled high on his plate

Unable to see clearly, make sense of it all

Consulted too many experts from the time he was small

With empty words, savant sounding, though no clarity was seen

The more words deployed to portray the obvious to any eye keen

The clearer it becomes what they hide, behind their science

'You're sick' say parents, teachers, psychiatrist – the unholy alliance.

It's true he lived in a world confusing and mean

Where his truth was different, so it had to be clean

Differences were pegged as wrongheaded, unmanly

Not like older brother, the pride of the family

Father was upright, Christian and strong

He knew what to do to be valued, and belong

But belong to what, at what cost to be paid

No thought was given, only that rules exist to be obeyed.

So he taught the elder son a man to be

Kill, compete, win, that's how in Texas a man is free

And his mother, somewhat deeper, played her part

Unhappy in her role, she always seemed slightly apart

But her softer side cried out for someone to love

Yet within God's rules, one must rise above

So the second son, her husband became

That seemed a fair bargain to her, it played the game

As much as older brother and father staked out their claim

They were the men, in behavior, outlook and name.

So what role, what place, remained for the younger of the two?

He was claimed by Mother, so what could he do?

Abandon his nascent manhood, that role was filled

Set out on a path where his manhood could only be killed

To assert his right to be himself in this world unforgiving

He made believe, a false life he was living.

Some were fooled, the façade held for a time

But at home, the men saw through it, and exacted a terrible fine

Both father and brother would turn out the lights

He was their prey, the hunted, the victim, caught in their sights

Like the deer fleeing his pursuers, to whom he did no wrong

His hide they would have, to them his skin would belong.

So run and hide, never knowing why

And mother, ultimately evil too, she watched him cry

More different, more frightened, more sensitive he became

A fortress he built of vigilance, anxiety was its name

For difference brings with it a curse unnamed

Conform, forget, give in and be tamed

But if you can't, if something deep from within says fight

Perverse ways of engaging emerge in the night.

Anxiety, fear, insomnia and more

Sex, substance abuse, betrayal all lie in store

For if one is so wrong in the eyes of the world

How could he stand tall with his flag unfurled?

The initial premise is false, yet the house he builds starts from there

Life offers no promise of salvation, of love, so why care?

Fighting each day exhausts every reserve

Death at times seemed the more attractive option – a preserve

A quiet place where the battle would cease

And a fantasy filled place would finally bring peace

To the outside observer, all of this is clear

And when explained in simple words, the obvious was near

But something arose from deep within

To look once again under the rock would be too great a sin

Not to place blame on parents or kin

To do so would risk rekindling the desire to win

But when you've been told all of your life

Even if acceptance has finally come, there will be no wife

No children, no future, no love, no hope

He could only struggle for some vague distant rope.

There is no one to turn to, no one to stand by his side

And even if there was, to believe, he could not abide

The fortress Anxiety, the one he never left

Has become a prison, there condemned, though he committed no theft

Caught between these forces which were once protective walls

Are now are so high, any hope of help sounds like empty echoes of distant calls.

DREAMS

Your dreams, those you've buried deep

The ones in your heart you are supposed to keep

Have you abandoned them one by one?

No father to help build them with his son

Another orphan in his place

Emptied of his own dreams, the blank face

But you, I feel your loss, given away

With no dreams, no future – a heavy price to pay

Only one at a time, each follow the other

With no soul, no joy, no loving brother

Immature you once suggested, a facile explanation

To dismiss your slowly sinking island nation

Something went amiss, something thrown overboard

Only left to serve an even emptier Dark Lord

Day in, day out, a heavy sameness abounds

With lost dreams, all that remains : infertile grounds

I know there is more, disappointments accumulate

Interpreted as sealing for you some unavoidable fate.

But I know of your joy, I've felt it live

You have so much more when you care to give

In ways that we spoke of, we shared, we knew

There was a time when your heart grew

Not ready to abandon you yet

Though try me you do, in your stubbornness set.

You think to control your heart by freezing it cold

When all it does is make you prematurely old

Cynical is for those who embrace hope that is lost

Too afraid to believe in their dreams, by life too violently tossed

But something survives buried within you deep

The hill to climb looks now perhaps too steep

But here I am, my hand always there

You know that with my help, you can dare.

Revive those dreams, feel the rush they provide

Step into the sunshine, you've no longer need to hide

You shackles of dark illusions, aside them cast

They live not in your future, but belong in your past

A new voice a new message, one in tune with your heart's current place

Though much time seems wasted, this is not some race.

But a quest, your salvation, the future you long to seek

The one that frightened you when you saw but a peek

Too close to the truth – your truth – you did come

Joy, excitement, love, fun

The world on its head, you chose dark over light

You put down your arms before you took up the fight.

Faith needs hope for a chance to survive

With the latter you buried the former alive

These are matters where logic has little sway

Emotions see more clearly, they point the way

Doubt leads to fear, fear abandons love

Yet when needed, like to Noah, comes the dove

Soft and gentle, not harsh or filled with hate

Brings back into focus the next gate

Imperfect, unsure, in uncharted land

Yet certain of the unfailing, caring, offered hand

Will it be taken, is the time now right

Or does darkness still obscure the light?

All I know is what I've said

How to stay alive, and not be dead

This is the way I know how to do

This is the way, tried and true

This is the way, my part I fulfill

This is the way, believe in a future or cling to the same tired old drill.

ABANDONMENT

March 4, 2013

As I've crossed life's waters in search of love

There were times when it felt right, like some custom made glove

I opened my heart, my soul, my mind

Thinking that this time I'd met my treasure, found my find.

In the beginning there was faith, there was trust

And in the moment's passion there was even innocent lust

It seemed the body knew only to speak the truth

Regardless of age, I felt again my youth.

Forgetful the heart when it once again believes

Before the axe falls and its time again to grieve.

How long does the honeymoon last from start to end?

Can the line of time be stretched, can it bend?

Or is it more about simply running its course

Place you bets, randomly, like on some unknown horse.

At first it seems all is true

The sun shines in your eyes and the sky is blue

But clouds appear though from whence they came

No real point of origin can one easily name.

For a soul is indeed a complex blend

Like some Gordian Knot, it has neither visible beginning nor end.

In those I've known and come to love

In those who seemed to fit like a velvet glove

The same cloud has ultimately taken shape

And in its aftermath my mouth remains agape.

How could I have not seen what was to come?

How could I have been so blind, so dumb?

But those who have known no love when young

Learn early on to only mimic many a song sung.

Like karaoke, they can the lyrics read

But the music escapes them, like some bloodless bleed.

Chameleons, change color, in spite of themselves

It's their nature to deceive like magical elves.

The hole in their hearts, through no fault of their own

The depth of which has come to be known

In moments rare and far between

Brief glimpses caught but rarely seen.

Never filled from the start, the hunger remains

Inexorably infecting others with their formless stains

To believe in love – their own or that of another

Be it father, sibling, wife, or mother.

Is a risk too great, caught between hope and despair

Only for themselves, no other, can they ever truly care.

So life becomes a struggle, a daily fight

To learn to live with this emotional blight

For without love, there's no courage, no faith, no trust

Intimacy a stranger, replaced by faceless, soulless lust

A thirst to be quenched for brief periods of time

To return again darker, like some deep sunk mine

But such is no answer, for the heart's hunger will always return

There is no salvation from its recurring burn.

Who would have thought that cold could sear so hot?

And that nothing could cook in this cracked pot

For that is what all abandonments mean

When all that's known of love is a frustrated dream.

How sad that there is but one cure

How to face such loneliness, how to endure?

But that is the point, for love comes to their soul

And for a time, it may even fill their bowl.

Partake they do, eating incredulously

Daring to briefly believe in such unfamiliar bounty.

If unloved from the start, how to explain?

The reprieve from alone bears no name

Can it last, could the crack finally seal?

But most of all, can love ever be real?

What of the real? Is it friend or foe?

Can I trust in it, or should I make it go?

How to convert the unbeliever?

The one who has lived their life an emotional underachiever

Who has never tasted the truth, only made believe

Always holding the escape card up their sleeve.

For when things start to become too real

When a wounded heart starts to truly feel

Fear grips their soul and turns them away.

Better to leave, too scarey to stay.

And what of the lover, the one who chose to remain

Who knows not how to treat love with disdain

Who believes in life and seeks not to complain

Who is close to emotion which helps to explain

That truth is the way, never to feign.

Holding on to what was good so it can remain

A chameleon is born to blend in

How could we call its very nature a sin?

But we are not speaking of lizards or toads

We are not speaking of randomly chosen roads

For the dye is cast early on

What should have been there is already gone.

Life is movement, each step ahead laid

Forward, not backward, but most of all neither stuck nor stayed

And this is how it comes to an end

When fear takes over and refuses to bend.

The unloved turn away, caught in some knot

Between what they want and they fear, they can't cook so they rot

Paralyzed, alone, confused and lost

Cheated in the beginning ordains a high cost

And the other, the one who was fooled once again

All he can do is pick up his pen

And try to imagine some way ahead

For after all is considered, done and said

The pattern is clear, it must be broken

For real this time, not another vain try, the truth must be spoken.

So if your heart feels empty because it was never filled

If it beats only hollow sounds, echoes stilled

Then what's to do to change your course?

How to break down the walls and with what force?

The question is complex, so must the answer be too?

Or is there something simple that you can do?

Solutions on paper may be described

And those who need to practice them easily ascribed

But make no mistake, no magic here exists

Implementation must proceed in starts and fits.

An empty heart to be filled makes one mistake

That to fill it up, someone else's love it must take

But that's the error, the fatal flaw

Ignoring life's fundamental law.

We cannot fill a void with love that's stolen

Another's goods will always leave beholden

Look deeper inside and break the round

That's driven you to a false search that's run aground.

Lives have been spent seeking only to take

When the answer resides in baking your own cake

In looking deeper within, the ingredients still there

It's about giving not taking, learning for another to care.

Juliet was right for all time

To heal oneself there's a simple line

"…The more I give, the more I have…" she said

And the matter was thusly put to bed.

To fill one's own heart can only be done from within

To take, not give, that is the sin

So those who suffer have got it wrong

They've been singing for years a misleading song

No faith have they in what's in their heart

And so they play the opposite part.

Is the circle so vicious that it cannot be stopped?

Is the bottle shut so tightly the cork can't be popped?

This is where character, courage and hope are required

To pull oneself out of the swamp wherein mired

An empty heart is selfish at best

And destined to fail every one of love's tests

Unless and until it turns around

And believes in the inner voice making another sound.

A call to believe, to cross the line

To take hold of the dream and to stop the whine

Step up and say ".. I care for another

You are my life, my dream, my other.

I will think of you as I think of myself

When it comes to a choice, you won't remain on the shelf.

And with each act of love the empty heart will fill

And the sum of hurt will decline on the bill

A day will come when this will change who you are

And the heart's waters will rise so high as to be seen from afar.

Full of love once again that no one can steal

For you will have learned something other than pain to feel."

You will own your heart, and no longer need to heal.

HANK

November 2015

Born into a world in constant turmoil

Where violence ruled, life lived at a boil

Unwanted, the result of who knows what

Emerged this child, as if from a pot.

Mother, young, deranged and drunk

Father, older, a crook, a skunk

Prior wives, other children came before

Made their way, luckier, they found the door.

A mistress on the side, part of the deal

Love? What's that? We're here to steal.

The rules – they are for others to heed

Not for them, on the honest ones they feed

The child, a boy, opened his eyes

And all he saw was anger, lust and lies.

The truth is for others, trust as well

A slow fall began into this hell.

The mother, disturbed, all substances she used

Surely in pain, unloved herself, deeply confused

Every frustration required someone to blame

With the birth of this boy, it now had a name.

Wrong in all cases, from the very first

An image began to take hold – he was the worst.

So began the story of his life

No peace to know, only constant strife.

Though born into this place where nothing good made sense

He was different, though damaged, his potential immense

But values take hold from what we observe and learn

And away from his true path he started to turn

Knowing the pain was through no fault of his own

Missing the warmth of love, dark seeds were sown.

Run, escape, thoughts to leave this hated place

Where to go for this was all he knew, his space

Surrounded by madness, it became a race

Orphaned three time by 13, he became a real hard case.

On his own too early, no home, no place

Run from the hurt, anywhere he could go

Neighbors, relatives, strangers he didn't know

Whoever would welcome this child of the dark

In spite of the shadows, there remained always a spark.

Yet learned he did, his welcome was never to last

So roots grew stunted, never fed, they learned to fast

The child grew up as best he could

Never taught right from wrong, bad from good.

But something inside kept it alive

Though it couldn't be trusted if he was to survive.

For growing up fat, food now love's surrogate

Picked on, no one to protect him, he found a new resource – hate.

Within the depths of his soul, a brother, a friend

Coalesced into a person, who was there to defend

Full of bluster, ruthless, primal and strong

He would be there to protect and belong.

This worked well for a time, as the boy, unguided, dabbled in crime

Trouble his vernacular, ever darker over time

Scam, lie, cheat and steal

That's how you live, who wants to feel?

Identities many, to the point of confusion

Slip through the cracks, life's but an illusion

The only constant, the protector, named Hank

Grew stronger, more dangerous, a human tank.

With defenses unbreachable, always ready when danger arrived

No doubt saved him often, that's how he survived

And so he sank further into despair and mistrust

The image others gave him, always deeper was he thrust.

Into becoming a part of the world from which he came

Reality, the future – it all was now a game.

How to beat the system, live between the lines

Trouble came easy, and so did danger at times.

But Hank would erupt, no limits he knew

Whatever was required, that's what he'd do

And with each instance, stronger he became

The boy knew Hank, but started to forget his own name.

Orphaned too young, three times in fact

Drugs were sold, for money he never lacked

During this time, work was found

Legitimate for awhile, he began to live on solid ground.

But that came to an end – screwed he would say

Trying to do good, he always seemed to lose the day

Money dwindled, work was not to be had

What was left but to give in, embrace the bad.

Mired in poverty, too proud to ask

What now must he do, what was his task?

The obvious escaped him, taught by the world he knew

No good could come from such a worthless crew

Go to school, some skills, the conventional way?

Always a reason "NO" to say

So deeper he sank, as in quicksand mired

His instincts kept him going, and he grew so tired

Of the worthless life, the struggle to fill each empty day

Cursed, he must be, that's what he'd say.

And when he met someone willing to be there

To prove to him that though not easy, it's possible to care

About oneself, and then another

To pick him up when he fell like a big brother.

But just when it looked like a he might let down his guard

Hank would return to drag him back to the yard.

Then the dark truth showed its ugly face

Life was always to be unforgiving, a cruel race.

For Hank had taken control, vigilant always

No sleep at night, no sleep during the days

Watch your back, look left and right

No telling who is out for you, fight or flight?

Gangland the country where he did reside

Danger was everywhere, no ebb or flow like the tide

Exhaustion growing each day, how long can he endure?

Is the outcome so certain, so dark, so sure?

I think the battle rages inside his soul

This other from a foreign world, has a goal

Salvation, what would that mean?

How far down a person's perdition can truly be seen?

No, what he knows is that good still lives on

If he stays the course, perhaps he'll finally see through Hank's con.

When a fortress, once protective, a prison becomes

When its high walls block out the hope and warmth of the stars and suns

When there seems to be no road ahead

When something breaks, light appears instead.

It's a slim chance but reason to hope

When seen with no filters, with reality we can cope

So chip away, one message sure and true

There still is good, from the beginning I knew

But the struggle isn't mine, it belongs to him

No longer fat or mocked, he is fit and trim.

So Hank's task is complete, his purpose fulfilled

But can he left go before his charge is killed?

To cede his place and let him live

Can Hank too love, a chance to give?

Or born of pain, anger and hate

Will he always stand guard, barring the gate?

More details could be told, as they were related to me

But enough has been said for others to see

The risks of placing oneself in a fragment's hand

The protector offers no Promised Land.

DARKNESS DESCENDS

May 2016

Darkness descends

Whilst he seeks to make amends

The pain from the past

A heavy pall is cast

Brief moments relief

From the core of grief

No love ever known

No seeds ever sown

Escape from the weight

Too heavy the gate

All help is in vain

Nothing but pain.

So lash out at the world when the mask grows heavy

Any small progress made, is taken - a levy

The future but an illusion

Everyone in collusion

Never wanted, never loved, never learned to care

How can one live in this world, how well can one fare?

If he doesn't believe

If all he knows is to grieve

If in his heart

The original sin writes his part

Each day to fulfill

Oh this bitter pill

Why fight, why learn, why dare to hope?

When it takes all his energy just to cope.

Each bridge is begun only to destroy

How can a man ever emerge from this boy?

Set him free, a guide I tried to be

To open his eyes, to make him see

So until that day, should it ever come

When he finds what it means to be a father, a son

Little hope this day will ever come

No joy, no love, alone, most likely, done.

God's anger in these souls an expression is found

For them there exists no hallowed ground

No salvation, no savior, though some have tried

Born in the wrong place, that day his future died.

WHAT I WANT

2016

What I want, what I need

Has nothing to do with money, status or greed

The most precious things money can't buy

Yet everyone thinks they can, so they try

But the reasons we care, the reasons we dare

Lie deeper inside, so life seems unfair.

No money, no job, no home, a troubled past

Seen through my eyes mean little , they're not meant to last

Unless we continue to let them define our path

It could go either way – just do the math.

I see within you who you should have become

Had life given you a good father, a good mother, and let you be a good

Son4

The one you truly wanted to be

But your past holds you tight and won't set you free.

When I see you, it's the healing you need

A starved heart requires a special diet on which to feed

To nourish, to restore those parts withered from neglect

And find the way back to health, love and respect

Unlock the door, let in the sun

Let trust bloom, and the war will be won.

You think with money, all problems are solved

That worthy you'll become, you will have evolved

From the misperception of a failed self

Who can only survive, living on someone else's shelf

Those are the values you've seen, you think they work

But they'd only turn you into another kind of a jerk.

Why did you touched me, why should I care?

Why persist, as on some mission, when your behavior is so unfair?

Is that when you allow yourself to simply be you?

To rise above the dirty, messy stew

I feel your goodness, the one you should now be

Why is it so unclear for you, yet so evident for me?

You were cast adrift too young with no defense

Who was to blame for this?   You? It made no sense

And so you learned to fight each day

To not get beaten up, mocked, shamed in some way

But deep down inside, the fears remained

Unspoken, untreated, unhealed – your heart was stained.

It must be your fault, you thought, this was to be your fate

To live in a world with no one to trust, such is to live in a world of hate

That blended well with you anger and rage

Revenge become your purpose, it had come of age

Where others lived in occasional violence as well

For you It became normal to live each day in hell.

Looking around, you saw ugliness all around

No one really protested, so the logic seemed sound

Doubts of your worthiness took hold, your sense of value was lost

Abandoned by love, that was to be the cost

But then through some strange twist of fate

I thought early enough, yet soon proved to be too late.

On the lowest day of your life, the dice – for real this time – you tossed

When no shred of hope remained and all seemed lost

You found your way to my door

Not knowing at all what might lay in store

You found a world you didn't know could exist

And someone who saw more in you, the ironic twist

That's often how it works, when at our lowest point

Life intervenes, with some hope your head to anoint.

But now a new challenge emerges, one you've never really faced

Finding what you've longed for, all the fear and failure - could it possibly be erased?

How scarey the prospect, to finally get what you've sought these many years

Yet something always blocks your path forward – it's all your old fears.

The hell you've known become too familiar, knowing well the rules

Though you also know they were written by morons and fools

But this new world, the one that draws you to places unknown

Though full of promise and hope, abandoning the past would leave you alone.

Could you trust my words to be true and that I would still be there?

Would I – like all the others – abandon you, or still care?

So back and forth between despair and hope

You spin your wheels and try to cope.

Two steps forward, one step back

The frustration builds on this narrow single track

Can one trust the winds to bring us home in a world tha'ts so new?

Could it be, a new life, is that true?

If the old rules no longer apply

Is the wind strong enough to carry the birds, can they still fly?

I have shown you in so many ways

That I have been here for you these many days

And I know you try, you struggle at great cost

The old voices tell you if you abandon them, all will be lost

They say stay in this hell, at least your place is assured

The disease in your heart can never be cured.

But that is a lie, darkness wants you to stay

She feeds on your despair each and every day

Starve her, deny her, turn your back and face the sun

Reject the fears she thrives on and you will have won.

No question, no doubt, a better life awaits

The monsters you see standing between you and the gates

Are only illusions, fears from the past

If you will them away, that day is their last.

Take this courage, and look deep within

You have not committed any fundamental sin

The reason those who should have loved you cast you aside

The sin is theirs, so the punishment too, in them – not you – should reside

See the goodness I've seen from the start

The sweetness, the calm, the innocence that lies in your heart.

These are the gifts you can give to me

These are the gifts no money can buy, they are free

For the more you give of the most precious in you

Each day, your life, you can renew.

Would you ever have thought such wealth you possessed?

That another's life, by your presence, could be blessed

These are truths I know to exist

Your gifts, they are many, too long here to list

Unbind your heart, your hands, your mind

The old world, the darkness, the fear – leave them behind

To heal your heart for me is the greatest gift

To no longer see you tossed on some cruel ocean, adrift

To watch you become who you were meant to be

For light to defeat darkness, a great victory

Assemble your strength, your courage, hold on to your trust

Stab your past in the heart with one lethal thrust

Do what you do then hold fast to its goodness, don't give in to doubt

When done with sincerity, it's your truth it's about

Each day think to give of your true gifts, the ones that are real

And know from them, the emotion, strength derives when love you feel.

Though new to you, untested and risky beyond current belief

Know that only from this can come your relief.

No safer place to test the ground will you find

To carry the day, use your head, your heart and your mind.

In the end, as is most often the case

Change may come at any pace

The result somehow preordained

In our very nature, ingrained.

When broken too early in life, the soul can rarely heal

Once living tissue has been forged into steel

Perhaps to survive there was no other choice

When a young heart is deprived of its voice

So build high the walls, reinforce the defences

Man the barricades, guard with your lives the fences

A breach in these ramparts would be fatal, the end

That is the message Control Central will send.

So wary of the dove announcing some hope

We've lived long enough to have learned with life's deceptions to cope

Deny them, fear them above all other things

For to let them in only destructions it brings

And so the world turns inside out

The friend, the ally, the hero now is seen like some stupid lout

Whose only goal is to lie, cheat and steal

While feigning a promise of what can never be real.

And so ends a journey, the fruit of some desperate search

The new foundations were laid to build a new church

But as darkness descends shutting out the light

The work is abandoned, and with it the fight

What looked briefly like the beginning of better days

The walls have fallen to the assault of the old ways

And as I look on the ruins of what might have been

I ask myself what I did wrong, where was my sin?

We, of the light, always look first ourselves to blame

Yet knowing that to in trying, there is no shame

But failure is indeed a bitter meal

Defeat cuts the cord, alone again we feel

And the other? Lost to a past too strong to change

Why bother if all our efforts only serve to derange

The answers seem clear, though insufficient to me

Both sides of the argument I see

Perhaps we don't really have a choice

And so I complain, vainly, yet still I will always raise my voice.

LOSS

CHANGES

October 2014

Can things we care for ever last?

Or must they always be lost to the past?

Though change is a part of life

Even the good things get cut off by the knife

Of time, ruthless and unforgiving

With little or no care for the living.

How to trust if everything must change?

A life to organize, build and arrange

When each and every one follows their way

Guided by some unseen hand, irrevocable, holding sway

And what makes it worse, to understand and accept

Our blindness to see what's ahead, away plans are swept.

Words mean nothing in the face of this

As faithless as a lover's kiss

Yet what choice do we have if life is so defined

But to stumble forward, nearly deaf or dumb, but blind.

When love arrives, a surge of faith takes hold

We go from uncertain and meek, to brave and bold

The skies seem to clear, obstacles shrink

That's how it appears, or so we think.

But over time, facades fall away

The deeper wounds surface and begin once again to hold sway

We talk, seek help, make believe we reflect

But the truth remains shrouded, obvious reality we neglect.

And though the same pattern may emerge, time and again

Even if we pick up the same paper and pen

It's too difficult, too painful for most to want to see

What's wrong, our share of blame, visible so obviously.

So focus as best we can, harsh truths we try to bring intoy to view

Hoping to build a future that's different and new

But wait, the equation has more than one part

One mind, one soul, one past, one heart.

.

Brought together by forces dark and unknown

The garment pieced with disparate elements, and with a thin thread sewn

It looks coherent, stylish and strong

It even seems to fit – for awhile – fostering a sense that together we belong

But time wears away the imperatives which bind

And soon we discover we are not of the same kind.

Now that is no task impossible to meet

In fact it's one of life's greatest adventures, one we should greet

To take two complex equations, blend them into one

Is it really like trying to meld the moon and the sun?

Are we really that different, that far apart

For we both share one necessity, a living heart.

But nowadays who has time or care for such things

When work, money, self gratification have been crowned our new kings

Not so grave this would be if it were only that

We've lost our compass and the world has become flat

Such simple matters as why I do what I do

Have now become unknowable, unspeakable, taboo.

Hard wired, genetics and neurochemistry

These are the new explanations, our blind Pharisees

Though they may suggest the how, no clue do they to the why

The important questions remain, address them we must try

But in the face of these static explanations, frozen in time

No more understanding have we gained, ignorance is just fine.

We name a thing and consider it done

But an illusion is what we've created. Ready now? Where's the fun?

For that's what's replaced true endeavor

More important to be amused than to ponder forever.

Lazy. Thoughtless. Empty. And lost

These are the price. This is the cost.

Is that why things change continuously

Escaping our control, breeding uncertainty

Only on the truth, whatever that may be

Can we build for what we consider eternity.

We've dealt the truth a vicious blow

Decided its essence impossible to know

It's been quantified, renamed, objectified and reduced

To something we barely believe in, sterile, deduced.

Through taking an interest in only what we can touch and see

We've thrown the rest back into the darkest sea

But if we never sought to look beyond what was near

We would never have escaped the time of darkness and fear.

Yet these days have returned, ignorance we seem to embrace

Pondering the unknown is once again too scarey to face.

So children, whatever their age, once again rule

As their time has come anew, long live the fool.

DOORS THAT OPEN

May 2014

Doors that open, doors that close

Why? One asks – no one knows

Or so they say, blind acceptance the rule

To reflect on the answer, why be a fool?

For to think deeply when no one cares

All one meets are blank empty stares

Safer to keep demons locked deep inside

From oneself it's always better to hide.

To know the truth, really see what is there

Would require one to truly care

But why in these times is care so hard to find

When we used to think it natural to be kind.

Other values have come and taken their place

It's no longer a walk, but a mindless race

And as we run towards the edge of the cliff

No sweet smell awaits, nothing, not a whiff.

So what to do, as emptiness fills our hearts

Devoid of substance, we simply play our parts

The solace some find in chemistry and smoke

Allows a pause, pass the pipe, take a toke.

Inhibitions drop, a bond starts to form

Reality fades, a connection is born

Emotions rise up from their prison dark and drear

The touch of the other, draw them near

Feel their skin, sense their touch

How is it that in everyday life they never feel this much?

Images arise, connections abound

A new lover, a friend, could possibly have been found?

The night passes in joining and bliss

Never before was such meaning put in, and found, in a simple kiss

Sweet dreams lift you soft and sweet

Two become one, for a time, do they meet

But the sun rises early, the lovers awake

Old walls reappear, our leave we take

With daylight old habits return

That glimmer of light can no longer burn

Deprived of the oxygen which gave it life

The hours old bond is cut with a knife.

Embarrassed to have been for a time so real

I first thought the experience was meant to heal

But one element required for this to be

To be willing to look in the mirror and truly see

What is possible when we open those doors

And set aside for a time prevailing mores

When it is again natural to be open, at ease

When it is again natural to want truly to please

When giving brings more than taking in

And vulnerability is no longer a mortal sin

To speak one's truth as if the most natural of things

And believe it's right for everyone, not just kings

No judgement, no fear, no disdain

No confusion, no shame, no regrets, no pain

But this time, this place here no longer is found

A cold rope surrounds the heart, tightly bound

What briefly was thought right, now considered wrong

There may be some music, but it contains no song

No words, no meaning, no message at all

Just noise, with decibels that senselessly rise and fall

Like the chat which has come real communication to replace

Words it may contain, but no sentiment, no grace.

And so products on a shelf we've become

Lost in the discarded packaging, the joy – there is none

Was it ever so different? Have we changed that much?

Was there a time when we spoke with a look, a kiss, a touch?

And if there was, will it ever return

Or must we learn to live in our new cold hell, a fateful turn

Where the sun fails our lives to warm, and the ice, so cold, instead, does burn.

BELIEVE

February 24, 2015

From out of nowhere the darkest of clouds appeared

Like some fire raging across the land, my heart was seared

Whispers of loss these past weeks spoken and I feared

Sensing its approach as it neared.

Take notice but little, not wanting to believe

Too soon again to start to grieve

Though she'd been with me for awhile

A unique blend of innocence and guile

The thought of my flower's spring coming to an end

Science unable the insult to mend

So what was left for me to do???

What arms do I have against a foe old, yet always new?

Only those that are mine, they reside deep in my chest

These are the ones I know best

My first thought is to my own promises broken

Have my sins, through her, been spoken?

God is there to hear it all

It's when we need him the most that we issue the call

No words come in answer, rarely clear at all

Up to us to see the ball rise or fall

I

They aren't sharp, lethal or mean

They come from the other side, where shines a light clean

In their own way they battle against the encroaching fate

How or why they may work, will they come in time or be too late?

We cling to the hope the outcome to change

Until the last moment, fate to derange

Yet knowing we've lost, translated to pain

Hope is gone, only emptiness to remain.

LILY

April 2015

She arrived in a crate in early spring

When the flowers were in bloom, and Life was King

Two bright young eyes peered out from the dark inside

Unsure yet curious, not really seeking to hide

I pulled her out and held her in my arms

Relaxed, confident, trusting – her irresistible charms

I felt her relax, confident in my touch

Who knew for how long, how much

She would be mine, stay in my life

A friend, a presence, a hope, no – not a wife

For what she was was essential and real

To look at her, touch her, to know her, to feel

There were times with her natural would anger me so

And now that she's gone, I regret each time I said "no"

But that isn't fair, to me or her

Though as I look back specifics start to blur

The world requires us ourselves to deny

Yet in obedience there was never a lie

She did what she wanted unless otherwise told

Even in her mischief she was sly yet bold

But her heart, was strong and filled with gold

She should still be here growing slowly old

But it wasn't to be as darkness came from nowhere

Ruthless, mean, no matter, no care

As illness progressed and she weakened more each day

I asked her to fight so with me should stay

And fight she did, though I can't imagine the cost

Never showing that she knew long before that the war was lost

And that last night, no more arrows to cast

As she struggled – for me – the inevitable to outlast

I felt him approach, yet with no material sign

Like a fog, a mist, no substance, unmistakably malign

As closer he came, I clutched her as close as I could

That was all I could do, all that I thought I should

But then I knew there was but one thing left to do

So I thanked her for fighting so long, for I knew

Why she had fought so bravely for so long

Why she had lasted, why she was strong

She had fought the demon, suffered for me

And so I thanked her and set her free

I felt her life taken from away

Only tears left for me to say

And helpless I watched Death suck the breath from her, awful to see

And to realize that what once was, never again will be

I held her body, still warm, yet lifeless, a shell

From so high to so low, my heart, it fell

There is no preparation, nothing to do

Even now, more than two months later, and though I knew

I grieve for what was taken to no purpose too soon

I ask the sun, the sky, the moon

Why from this world of darkness, such beauty to take

Do you not, in this world, have a stake

To strike a balance, to give us hope

How to fight evil, how to cope

I know there is no ready answer, now reply on the way

But my heart cries, and it must have its say

So thank you perhaps for having had her for a time

To have felt the love she gave and that she was mine

But I cannot accept the way she was taken

By the light, at the end, she was forsaken

So Lily, my flower, for that's what you were to me

All sweetness and love and mature femininity.

THREE MONTHS

February 24, 2015/July 2015

From out of nowhere the darkest of clouds appeared

Like some fire raging across the land, my heart was seared

Whispers of loss these past weeks spoke and I feared

Sensing its approach as it neared

Took notice but little, not wanting to believe

Too soon again to start to grieve

Though she'd been with me for awhile

A unique blend of innocence and guile

The thought of my flower's spring coming to an end

Science unable the insult to mend

So what was left for me to do?

What arms do I have against a foe so old, yet always new?

Only those that are mine, they reside deep in my chest

These are the ones I know best

I fought with my love, my faith, my heart

We both did our best, each played their part

But a third, a stranger, did fast approach

Ethereal he came, not in car or coach

Not to be seem, yet his presence was felt

Against him we tried, yet in the end we knelt

None can resist his embrace, though insubstantial he appears

For he draws his strength from the sum of all fears

So late one night, sleepless I held her in my arms

And watched him suck her life away, with all her charms

I hope to never again live a similar event

I see it again, the image never exhausted or spent

Acceptance is all that remains for me to do

So drink I must from the bitterest cup, this foul, unholy brew

Perhaps a day will come when the hurt will go away

When I can think of her and smile – my pain having had its say

Three months have slipped away

I do what I must and get through each day

I laugh, I smile, I live as I must

The only way to fight him is in life to trust

For he will do his work, perhaps no one gave him a choice

Who would want his job, no body, no love, no voice

Only a presence one senses near the end

Without warning he comes, no messages does he send

And take what he wants, deserving or not

To his home underground, where precious souls are left to rot

I look to the sky, blue and clear

I chase away the clouds, banish my fear

But he is as real as anything born in the sun

In death can there ever be life, love or fun?

No answer have I found, though speculate I can

I must be brave, optimistic – I am a man

Once seen, however, the memory of him will never leave

So I try and find in my heart a corner safe and sure

Where her memory can live, prosper and endure.

SIX MONTHS HAVE PASSED

September 22, 2015

Six months have passed since you went away

The pain endures, no words can sway

The little things in life we shared

Without you here, my heart is bared

I keep busy with the baby in all her deeds

I smile and rage, my day she feeds

I sleep at night, thoughts elsewhere

Then I wake, you're missing, it's so unfair

An emptiness seizes me for a time, intense yet brief

Reason saves me, brings me momentary relief

I walk the streets we shared every day

Part of me in the present, part of me away

To that place where you lived and brought me light

Though absent, I still feel your light

And that last night, the one which will haunt me forever

I wish I could forget, yet I cling to it like a tether

The last string connecting me to you

My heart believing if I don't let go, you'll appear anew

Your courage, your strength, the love that lived in you

I reach for you in the night, absent, what can I do?

So I carry on, embracing life's gifts

My steps grow broader to bridge the rifts

The bad things which seem to come in spite of me

A change has come to the world, yet I cannot see

Where is the door, the new one I'm supposed to take

Every intiative taken turns out to be another fake

Depressed? No. Sad for both you and me

The waves washed the past away and swept you out to sea

I need to cry from time to time

They say tears heal, and may reveal a sign

Little solace Life wastes on we all

We rise, we move forward, we get stuck and we fall

But mark my way, though I don't know where it goes

You brought me highs, I must endure the lows

Do I cry for me? Do I cry for you?

All I know is that you were cheated and didn't get your due

So now the tears have come, I feel some relief

I don't know more so must rely on the belief

That you are cared for wherever you are

That he who took you away from me to a place too far

One I can't imagine, no matter how I try

Perhaps not knowing is why I cry.

The seas of my heart have calmed for now

Perhaps a restful sleep to allow

But know, wherever you are

If you are near or if you are far

You are as alive to me as you ever were

And the memory of you my heart will always and forever stir.

More tears I have – who knows how deep is the well

Time only knows an in its way it will tell

Will this pain ever leave me in peace

Will some gift of love bring me release

If I am to be blessed in this way

Hear me clearly, this I say

The core of us all is one single place

Back to this source, everything can be retraced

And for now this core, the center of my heart

Bears one face, one touch that can never be broken apart.

GONE

January 2016

It's almost a year now that Lily is gone

There are days when I get by, not put upon

But this grief, this need to cry my loss

There can be no doubt who is the boss

It seems there's no end to the tears

Nor purpose to all of these useless fears

I search for a reason why time has not healed

This wound each time fresh itself is revealed

I hope she's found peace in a better place

Where squirrels abound and she can race

Each memory brings pain, not peace as it's supposed to do

I drink from the cup each day my bitter brew

I am not alone and have others to love

Yet the last night when she died grips my heart like a glove

I set her free then from the promise she made

The courage and dignity, in the face of death, so composed, so staid

I need some reason perhaps to move on

And accept the unfairness of life and this world we stride upon

Is that the message, though struggle I may

To strive to live up to what I feel is important, to have my way

Is life punishing my hubris, my arrogant stance?

Is she laughing at me as I continue my dance?

I'm no longer sure why, I feel mostly pain

That's how he works, Death is his name.

TEARS

November 2016

Your picture as a puppy looks into my soul

It's as if you were alive, healthy and whole

Tears well up, so much in your eyes do I see

The bond is still strong between you and me

But why after all this time do I cry each day

When will this sadness, this pain ever go away

Do I keep it alive a means to keep you near

If I stop, will I forget, is that my fear?

I've lost loved ones in years gone by

But time healed the wounds, and the tears went dry

Yet Lily, my flower, who no longer lives by my side

I know you are gone, from this truth I can't hide

So hold on to you still, in spite of the pain

Will I ever feel your presence, your love, again?

I know the answer, though resist Death I may do

I'll pay this price daily, for me, for you.

YESTERDAY, TODAY, TOMORROW

THE OUTLIAR

January 2016

We are all born different, none come from the same place

Raised to enter, some to win some to lose, the same race

Why is it then, such a difference in pace

Look back on the road taken to find the trace.

Back to a time before things were stripped away

More is taken from us than is allowed to stay

Transformed by the years, demands are made

Survival always exacts a price to be paid.

What becomes of those pieces we too easily reject

Like defective software, the missing parts do have an effect

Should we think that these gaps make us less than should be

Or perhaps good guidance from our primal side, they'll set us free.

I have no definitive answer, but this I've seen

In those I've met, the cost has been mean

For from the darkness, the primeval slime

We did emerge over time.

Drag ourselves out of the mud, see the sky

Our spirits were born to teach us to fly

To aim for the stars knowing we'd never arrive

The point being perspective and a means to strive.

The conflict, the tension between light and dark

Can't really be separated in life, like tree and bark

One faces outward, protection and form

Collectively we've defined a new concept, the social norm

Norms and their cousin – normal - are cardinal points

Conform closely, some believe, our heads it anoints

Yet what became of those parts thrown away

Did they disappear or did they find a place to stay?

Like most that's rejected, It's tossed out of sight

To live in darkness, deprived of the light

That's the point, out of sight, forgotten, doesn't bring to an end

We don't know who goes on under the rock, we just pretend.

Those pieces, our "imperfections," early on maligned

Cry out for freedom, their place once again to find

Unfair, misunderstood, unjustly cast off with no potential appeal

If that happened to you, how would you feel?

Wounds fester in darkness, growing bitter, but can they heal?

Quite to contrary, anger and resentment these are the Gods to whom they kneel

Instead of rising up they sink back I the mud, their values evolve

Revenge appears to be their only resolve

But wait, this is still me, do I chase my own tail

If that is the case how can I but fail

Stuck, conflicted, silent enemies ignoring each other

One deaf, one mute, two sons born of the same mother

Who surely had her favorite, wanting only the best

Where would the wisdom come from if the survived the test?

Tell one to think back on the road from the start

Were there not moments when one became two, somehow torn apart?

At war with oneself, how could that be?

Forgotten these days past, or massaged into a convenient story.

Why bother with the past? We can't go back

It is what it is, too late to tack

To find a new wind, one fresh coming from behind

But wait, that's the same as the past, what to make of this find?

Could it be that that this wind comes from the original place?

The one where I started, lost in the race

It blows to remind me there's more to me than I know

Find a way to hear it so once again I can grow.

Away from this dead end, this rut we too often feel

Brother to brother, together we can heal?

Outliars are what we are from the day we are born

And as we live, from us vital parts are torn

Not all are good, some primitive and vile

"I was never perfect," to be repeated daily with a knowing smile.

But these things no one wanted in me

Are nonetheless deserving, if whole I am to be

So search for the wisdom, let in the light

Brothers shouldn't be enemies, nor should they only fight.

Light and dark, the contrast, strikes us as irreconcilable

Binary thinking, is simply too often unreliable

They mix, they blend, producing nuance and more

Suddenly a new direction appears, with much more in store.

A new ally, a friend, someone bringing fresh thought

A richness, a perspective, an opportunity – these things can't be bought.

So look back on the road traveled, much it explains

Don't be afraid of old wounds, or their accompanying pains

Wounds heal, pain passes, more clearly the present we see

And the future, the new choices I've sensed, are there to set me free.

FROM THERE TO HERE – AND BEYOND

January 31, 2017

It Is often thought – if thought at all

How life progressed, or did it stall?

Was it ever a journey and not a metaphor?

Was there a light guiding us towards some door?

All I had to do was follow it with never a thought

As to what my choices, my actions, were, a future I'd bought

I look around me and listen with care

Vague complaints resound how things aren't fair.

For we seem to live in the present, that's partly true

But would I have done otherwise, if only I knew?

If I could look back to the past and identify my faults

Instead of locking them away in our mind's many vaults.

To accept the blame for what has transpired

We're too busy, too lost, and oh so very tired

Yet life is full of ease compared to the past

So why do so many rise in the morning wishing it might be the last?

That thought evaporates quickly, it fills us with dread

So we dive back into the pool of confusion, if not our bed

It seems the cycle shortens with each passing year

And with it some vague anxiety replaces our fear

The objectless cause which we can't quite nail down

A pill, it seems, is the only thing that can banish the frown

For if we don't know the where's and the why

We live rudderless, blind, so why even try?

God gave us a mind – as he did to all things

So we could find our way and minimize life's stings

But this gift comes with a condition, nothing of great value should ever be free

We must live our lives sighted and strive to be "me"

So there is a direction to be found, all I need do is look

And remember my path is a story, a journey, a book

Each book has a plot, a narrative, a line we can trace

It started long ago in some distant place

And along the way, as time passed by

Choices were made, but how hard did we try?

Within our means at the time, did our options we consider?

Or did we let the win go to the lowest bidder?

The one who offered an effortless choice

The one where we listened to some other voice

Drowned out was the other whose words came from within

Why try so hard when easy awaits – is that not a sin?

Advancing thusly, consider the cost

What did we learn to inform our path forward, and what was lost?

Building a future on such flimsy ground as this

What chance did we have but to score a miss?

Such errors as these are not isolated in time or space

They burden us with doubt as we enter the race

Victories may come from time to time

But do they not belong to randomness, they surely cannot be mine,

For what did I contribute to make it so?

Did I prepare the soil, plant the seed, care for it so it might grow?

As the years passed, and choices accumulate

If I played no active part, who else can I blame but fate?

If I've built no certainty, no confidence in my ability to discern

And with each event, diminished the possibility to learn

Hopeless is it now to reset our course?

Is the only treatment for the challenges of marriage a divorce?

Once we realize that our life is a story with a beginning and an end

That the journey is not always easy and the road does bend

If we look back with brave eyes, willing to see

How from yesterday today came to be?

The turns in the road, the exits missed and undesired destinations

Together start to make sense and how our lives are our own creations

The difference becomes clear if a new way is sought

How to live our lives we were poorly taught

But now is a chance to take stock of the who and the what

Once we understand today from the why, a future we've begot

Clarity replaces confusion, anger, unavowed cedes it place to a more benign emotion

The ignored storm calms the waters of the ocean

The fog lifts, the sirens grow quiet

Ceding my role no longer a steady diet.

We see the tillar, unfamiliar with our hand

A new day can be born if we but take an enlightened stand

No more false Gods in whose name we claim to believe

Lost no longer in pain and confusion, we can cease to grieve

For what we gave up unknowingly at first

Not realizing for what it was that we had such a thirst

A cup in hand, filled by a present mind

This must be the way of all creation and humankind.

THE AMERICAN DREAM

February 2017

As a child of the 50s, grown up in this country

I benefitted from the expansion, the wealth, the bounty

The struggles of earlier times were wiped away by the war

Prosperity on the horizon, that's what we had in store

But was that the American dream, one of unbridled wealth

Was there something else lurking, operating by stealth?

Looking back to the promise this country offered the world

A gift of the Enlightenment, knowledge's flag unfurled

To point to things higher, not mundanely venal

Most were born to be free, not of a colony penal

Liberty. Freedom. Justice for all

These were the things, the purpose, the dream, the call.

We started out near the bottom, arrogance a creature from across the seas

There was much to do, so we set to work, like a human swarm of bees

Building this country, with purpose and a dream

No time to inflate ourselves, nor to be greedy or mean

But something happened, brought about by success

We started to want more, and thought of giving back less

After World War II, having defeated Depression and War

We had won, so surely, such accomplishments promised an open doo

r

One to a future, first rewarding our innate nature, so great

The future was by definition ours, so much to do, and not to be late.

Achievements in science, the arts, commerce and trade

Nothing to limit our appetites, to us nothing forbade

This new American Dream emerged from a myth, which is not the same thing

We'd forgotten how came our success, what we did that made us king

For kings can be born, having no merit to justify their station

Or they can serve the values that gave birth to a great nation.

So onward we climbed the ladder of power and wealth

And lurking in the shadows this dark creature who operates by stealth

More riches came, but problems too

Complexities hounded us, they were many, not few

Size breeds complications, and here we prefer answers that come soon

That don't require too much thought, time is money and money is a boon

It's the thing that we've come to cherish above all other things

And those original values have sunk back in the swamp with the discord it brings.

Unable to solve problems – practical one's preferred

Throw money at them, from easy solutions we will not be deterred

But as our inherent goodness started to falter and fail

A challenge to our self-image, seeds of doubt took root, we started to grow pale.

But this is a country built nowadays on superficialities and easy solutions

Having lost our way, those elevated values lost their power, now weak dilutions

Empty words enshrined in meaningless speeches

Politicians breed in the swamps, like so many leeches

And the great American populace, we who saved the world time and again

Retained the myth, but not the dream, all these problems, what a pain

But as long as I was alright, what care have I for the others?

This country was built by each individual, with no help from sisters or brothers

Titans of industry tout self-reliance and strength

Success awaits for those who will go to almost any length.

But we forget the collectivity, for each giant stands of solid ground

Protections, advantages, facilities, all abound

So the myth grows more misleading with each generation

And in the end, we have no north star, only an hollow nation

One that believes the fallacies it tells itself each day

Fear and anger have taken hold, nothing good to say.

Like the children who bicker when things go wrong

We look for someone else to blame, that's our new song

For to look in the mirror and see who might just be at fault

Take that thought quickly and lock it fast away in a vault

So here we are, with a President who should never have been

Fingers of blame pointed at the weak, the Other, thrown them into the bin

For they are the cause, criminals, rapists, drug dealers and more

Send them home and slam the door.

For we are the best, by definition, none can contest

I will stand tall, tell everyone who'll listen, better than all the rest

Safe in our ignorance, comforted by myths and smoke

Certainty belongs onty to those who are intellectually broke.

Things have begun to fall apart, of that we are sure

I only care about me, someone bring me the cure

For all this greatness has come without us understanding why

When things go wrong, all we know is to look angrily at the sky

Demobilized, depressed, drugged up to the hilt

It's societies fault, I have no guilt

I am the victim, though there too, I refuse the name

So, I'm a hero, hard-working, screwed over – that's the new game.

I'll follow any pied piper who promises a return to some non-existant past

When everything was great, and we were sure no effort was required for it to last

By what magic can the past be brought back today?

By what magic will I get my job back now that's its gone away?

By what magic will I have money for cars and tv's like it used to be?

By what magic will I no longer be unemployed and 53?

Suddenly, inexplicably the dream has dissolved into the lie it always was

What did Forrest Gump say – stupid is as stupid does?

The writing was on the wall so many years ago

We saw it coming but chose not to know

How could a country as great as ours fail?

How could my life crumble and end up in jail?

My house lost to the bank, the car repossessed, bankrupt and lost

Such is what happens to those who close their eyes, such is the cost.

Is anger and frustration, blaming others, choosing leaders who lie through their teeth

Who profess to tell the truth, but hold no knowledge – only conviction and belief

The answer is there, waiting to be found

There still remains in the country much fertile ground

What we need to do is learn to think once again

To get out of our homes, now less a castle than a play pen

To look to the sky, as founding fathers did long ago

And recall what the American Dream was about, and start once again to sow.

The seeds of freedom, of liberty, justice and the like

And lose the epithets of niggers, latino, muslim and kike

For we rise and we fall together as one

If we do, a new day awaits, announcing the return of the Sun

But if we continue down this road of selfish abandon

We can say good-bye to "Hot" and "Fun"

If we continue to act as children, who think in terms of pleasure today

The sky will grow dark, and the Dream will go away.

SMOKE

March 1, 2017

Smoke appears asf a contradiction

We see it, smell it, yet by its ephemeral nature, is it reality or a fiction?

It appears when something goes from solid to volatile

The physical transformation replaces substance with style

Fascinating to watch it rise and disperse in the air

A short lived pleasure to enjoy without a care.

That's how we look at things, once they are out of sight we can forget

So much has just happened, yet its disappearance removes all – even regret

No need to consider potential effects

Dilution solves all problems, as our thinking it corrects.

Only children believe things don't disappear when they vanish from sight

So why worry about smoke, given time all things come right

Smoke has another function, it can induce a certain state

Of relaxation and confidence, enhancing our ability to relate

And if the words sound soothing, no need to think

Give me some more, and how about that drink?

Yeah – that sounds right – what did he say?

No matter, all heads are shaking in approval day after day

Smoke is the stuff myths are made from

No substance to check, repetition validates like the beat of a drum.

Myths are enhanced versions of how ourselves we want to see

Inspiration can come too, that's how we want to be

Dreams of betterment, progess awaits

Keep our eyes on the target, I see the gates.

But myths, though stories, filled with instruction

Like smoke, also imply a preliminary destruction

And that period in between when solid is transformed

So too truth about ourselves can be deformed.

Caught up in the race, we tend to forget

The values guiding us also serve as a safety net

And as we approach this better place

Instead of the target, I see more my own face

For I have achieved so much, or so I'm told

I've become blind as well as bold

Perspective is lost, confusion ensues

Reality recedes as advances alternate news.

Solids lose their substance, judgement defers

Give me more smoke as my vision blurs

Mesmerized by the shifting patterns I see

Ignoring our challenging reality now becomes easy.

Words flow to reassure – a form of smoke

No need to inhale to take a toke

We gladly inhale as we slowly go broke

And I'm not talking of weed or coke

I'm talking about withdrawing from life, taking a pass

As we collectively indulge ourselves, blowing smoke up our own ass.

CASUAL-TY / FORMAL - ITY

March 2017

An evolution, a process exists in human kind

Hand in hand it progressed favoring the human mind

Rigid rules guided all things

From chieftans to nobles to queens and kings.

These rules brought hierarchy and structure, established order

Separation a necessary component to calm disorder

Nations fought wars, cruel for little sense

The world was wild, unbridled, immense.

Once things took shape and cultures established

How then to keep things from coming unmeshed

Formality, a word we use less and less

Clearly informed each one's place, keeping away the mess.

Stratified societies, diplomatic practice, courtesy – all held fast

Estates, nobility, clergy, peasants – each belonged to some caste

Organization thus established, all bowed to the unstated form

Interiorized, it all just seemed natural, the glue, the norm.

With order came growth bringing prosperity and wealth

Formality held firm, in silence and stealth

But man is an acquisitive being, always wanting more even with enough

Never to be satisfied, be it through envy or desire, he hungers for more stuff.

The rules, they were strict, break them and see

Pressures were building, some new space to bend them, flexibility

So bows to one's lord, service given without question

Started to wear on the social digestion.

Measures were taken in the name of values we cherish

Once pressure builds too high, its adapt or perish

Equality, freedom, individual choice, democracy

Each individual part started to claim their personal liberty.

The web that held it all together for so long

In this new order, the old rules no longer seemed to belong

Technology brought progress, modernity too

Opening up the former privileges, in earlier times reserved for the few.

Wars of horrific scale, progress' levy

The price in suffering was indeed heavy

When the smoke cleared and the dead were buried

The old order was simply gone, to Hades ferried.

And what emerged, a new world that was missing its old head

No longer in charge, all were glad they were dead

But who was to rule, ensure order in their place

A crown might exist, but who was to wear it, what was their face?

The people, the masses, the liberated us

No more reserved seats on the zero privilege bus

Busy with rebuilding the world we'd just nearly destroyed

Hope and enthusiasm, all were buoyed?

So much to do, so many dreams to fuilfill
No more time to indulge the ever present desire to kill
All could speak their minds, regardless their station
Equal we all were in this new modern nation.

Things got raucous, conflicts or another type took form
They looked different for the old rules were no longer the norm
Disorganization, deconstruction, civil rights ruled the day
If all equal, then all are entitled to an equal say.

All would be good except for one fact
We all didn't start from zero and to deal with that, how do we act?
Competition. Capitalism. Let the markets decide
A nice fig leaf to cover this detail to hide.

So the rules became written, decided by compromise and consent
To accommodate all, clauses were included to allow them to be bent
And with each new law a new loophole was born
No single truth, like some holy cloak, could be worn.

The truth became the subject of dispute and dissent

Until now, it seems, it's become totally irrelevant.

How to summarize what has taken centuries to come to pass

What force can we name that gave the power to the mass.

If rules give rise to values, or the opposite be true

We live by them with each passing year to a lesser degree – who knew?

Some can characterize it as narcissism – it's all about me

Others may not even think that far, I can do what I want, I am ME.

If we all sink or we swim as one, united or not

If there's to be food to eat for all or nothing in the pot

Something must emerge, a new consciousness like glue

For if its all about me, who could possibly care about you?

Formality was a way of life which brought structure and order

Though imperfect, it established society and all its borders

The countervailing force, necessary for progress

Relaxed the rules, its name casualness.

As with all things bipolar, the pendulum swings

Never stopping in the middle, some long lasting peace to bring

The tension is necessary for mankind to evolve

And if done knowingly, wisely, collectively, our problems we will solve.

But beware the extremes, lethal they can be

Open your eyes, think, see

Or sweep all the good we've done into the abyss

For then there will so very much to miss.